❦ June ❦
2003

Dear Doreen,

... I wish we could
have shared more
time, more memories
together here in London...
One year is not
enough ... Good luck
I will miss
you
Colleen

$\frac{1}{7462}$

$\frac{1}{9218}$

$\frac{1}{7677}$

$\frac{1}{7004}$

$\frac{1}{9188}$

$\frac{1}{9243}$

$\frac{1}{8957}$

$\frac{1}{7578}$

Where to Take Tea

**A GUIDE TO OVER 50 OF THE BEST PLACES,
FROM VICTORIAN TEAROOMS TO GRAND HOTELS**

SUSAN COHEN

This book is dedicated to my mother, Edith, who loved Fullers' Iced Walnut Cake.

First published in 2003 by
New Holland Publishers (UK) Ltd
London • Cape Town • Sydney • Auckland

Garfield House
86–88 Edgware Road
London W2 2EA
www.newhollandpublishers.com

80 McKenzie Street
Cape Town 8001
South Africa

Level 1, Unit 4
14 Aquatic Drive
Frenchs Forest, NSW 2086
Australia

218 Lake Road
Northcote
Auckland
New Zealand

1 3 5 7 9 10 8 6 4 2

ISBN 1 84330 215 2

Senior Editor: Clare Hubbard
Design: Cube
Editorial Direction: Rosemary Wilkinson
Production: Hazel Kirkman

Reproduction by Modern Age Repro, Hong Kong
Printed and bound by Times Offset (M) Sdn Bhd, Malaysia

Contents

Author's Foreword

RESEARCHING and writing this book has been a labour of love for me. Friends and family often ask me how I came to write it, given that my time is usually divided between working as an interior decorator and undertaking academic historical research. In all honesty, it came about by accident rather than design, but can be blamed on my love of social history, a chance encounter with some fascinating teashop archives and my enjoyment of scones and afternoon tea. The final outcome was this nostalgic, illustrated social history of tea and a guide to over 50 of the best tea venues in Britain, from fine hotels to cosy teashops.

Thanks are due to so many people, but a special mention must go to my editor, Clare Hubbard, who has coped brilliantly with my endless emails and has been a great help. To all the lovely people whose tea I have tasted and whose scones I have eaten, a big thank you. Regular walking with some good friends has helped me keep the extra pounds at bay and thanks, once again, to my husband, Andrew, whose unfailing support never ceases to amaze me.

Lastly, I hope that you gain as much enjoyment from reading the book as I have from compiling it.

Introduction

*If you are cold, tea will warm you –
If you are too heated, it will cool you –
If you are depressed, it will cheer you –
If you are excited, it will calm you.*

MR WILLIAM E. GLADSTONE
BRITISH PRIME MINISTER (1809–98)

QUEEN Victoria's Prime Minister, William Gladstone, captured the very essence of tea when he wrote these words in 1865. Relaxing, refreshing, stimulating or warming, there is little to compare with the comfort and delights of a steaming pot of tea. There is a certain magical, even mystical quality about tea, not least of all because of the amazing influence the tiny leaf exerts on everyday life. A cup of tea is the best reason in the world to stop for a break during the day. Life's rites of passage would not be the same without tea, and the variety of leaves is such that every mood and taste can be catered for. As the world's most popular drink, tea crosses all the boundaries of history, nation, culture and class. At some time in their lives, most people, even the smallest child, acquire a "taste" for tea, a habit that they rarely relinquish. Whilst the paraphernalia and rituals surrounding tea have a tantalizing effect on collectors, connoisseurs and the merely inquisitive, the social aspects of tea-drinking are fascinating and evocative of leisure and pleasure. Why not relax with a cup of tea whilst you read on…

William Gladstone's eulogy on tea (above left) was paired with this illustration and made into a postcard.

The Story
Of Tea

*Tea has a fascinating history. Its story is intertwined with
social trends and political events throughout the world,
from the Japanese tea ceremony to the Boston Tea Party.
Throughout its history it has been at the centre of people's lives,
whether for comfort during wartime, as a partner to the
tango or simple refreshment at a welcoming tearoom.*

How it All Began

Where better to begin than with an introduction to the fascinating story of how tea-drinking began in the East and then travelled to the West.

Origins in the Orient

THE story of tea-drinking began, as legend has it, as long ago as 2737 B.C., when the Chinese Emperor, Shen Nung, accidentally discovered the delights of camellia leaves – a relative of the tea leaf – steeped in hot water. However, centuries passed before the Chinese took to grinding up the leaves and whisking them in hot water or making flat cakes from them. The era of the Ming Dynasty, between 1368 and 1644, seems to have been a turning point in the history of tea-drinking, for it was during these years that the more familiar method of brewing leaves in hot water became a favourite pastime. The Oriental influence on tea

grew once the beverage travelled from China to Japan, for the Japanese turned tea-drinking into a celebration and honoured it with an elaborate ceremony.

Britain and Tea

WHEN tea was first introduced into Britain, it was known by its Cantonese name, *ch'a*, but after Britain's trading base was moved from Canton to Amoy (Fujian Province, China) at the end of the seventeenth century, the drink acquired a new and more familiar name, *tay* and later *tee*.

The British upper classes got their first taste of tea in around 1645, when the East India Trading Company introduced it to the country. Britain's monopoly on the export of the leaf meant that it was an expensive and scarce commodity, made even more so by the 119 per cent tax rate imposed by King Charles II's parliament. Very few ordinary people could afford to buy the leaf but this suited a number of groups – brewers, church leaders and medical men – very well. The brewers feared that "the meanest families, even the labouring people in Scotland [would] make their morning meal of tea to the disuse of ale". Leaders of the Church of England treated the Eastern provenance of tea with suspicion and concluded that it led to sin, whilst doctors – who actually knew very

> ### Japanese Tea Ceremony
> *The basis of the modern tea ceremony was established by Murato Shuko (1422–1502), renowned for his design of the 3-metre square (9-foot square) Japanese tearoom. He was the first person to make tea in front of his guests. At the heart of the tea ceremony are the four principles of wa-kei-sei-jaku, – harmony, respect, purity and tranquillity.*

This set of three silver tea caddies in a contemporary case date back to 1739.

little about medicine at this time – were certain that tea made people ill.

Scarcity and price made tea the ultimate status symbol and a fashionable luxury. It was given the royal seal of approval by Catherine of Braganza, the Portuguese wife of King Charles II, as she brought a chest of tea with her as part of her dowry in 1662. Little did she know how much solace she would find in her cup of tea, which she sipped whilst her husband frolicked with his favourite mistress, Nell Gwyn. Meanwhile, tea smugglers did a roaring trade and rich ladies became so protective of the luxury leaf that they kept it under lock and key in a stylish tea caddy – perhaps made by the celebrated English cabinetmaker, Thomas Chippendale (1718-79). Unlocking the caddy was as much a part of the ritual of

> 66 *Strong tea and scandal –*
> *Bless me how refreshing.* 99
>
> **THE SCHOOL FOR SCANDAL** *1777*
> *THE FAMOUS PLAYWRIGHT, RICHARD BRINSLEY*
> *SHERIDAN, MIGHT WELL HAVE WRITTEN THESE*
> *WORDS FOR QUEEN CATHERINE.*

serving tea to their guests as were the frivolous diversions of cards and music.

The tea scene in Britain changed dramatically because of events in America in 1773. History recalls how the colonial population, tired of the tax on tea, took it upon themselves to break the East India Company's long monopoly. Bedecked in native Indian outfits, large crowds unceremoniously dumped the tea cargo into Boston harbour in protest at the company's profiteering. The Boston Tea Party, as it became known, was one of the events that led to the American War of Independence.

Tea cargo being dumped into Boston harbour.

However, the most radical change to tea-drinking habits in Britain occurred in 1784 when William Pitt (1759–1806), then Prime Minister of Britain, finally reduced Chancellor of the Exchequer Cromwell's tax on tea to 12 per cent, making the beverage affordable by rich and poor alike. Tea became the drink of the masses.

Buying and Selling Tea

ONE of the first people to realize the potential of buying and selling tea was Thomas Garway, the owner of Garraway's Coffee House in Cornhill, in the City of London. He organized the earliest recorded London tea auction, in Mincing Lane in 1657. The following year the unnamed owner of another coffee house, The Sultaness Head, placed an advertisement in a popular news sheet offering "China *Tcha*, *Tay* or *Tee*" for sale. Until 1826 tea was always sold loose, by weight, but John Horniman, a merchant on the Isle of Wight, changed this when he had the novel idea of selling small quantities of leaf tea made up in labelled packets.

The Victorians owed a huge debt to Thomas Lipton, an entrepreneur who learnt the ins and outs of the tea trade in America before opening up his first shop selling tea in Glasgow in 1871. By 1900 his empire had grown to 100 shops and he was selling a million packs of the exotic commodity annually. Affordable tea was now widely available across Britain, with the "Lipton" name associated with tea throughout the world.

It was not only hot tea that became a firm favourite. In hot climates iced tea makes a very refreshing drink, as tea merchant Richard Blechynden discovered at the World's Fair in St Louis, America in 1904. During the heat wave no one was interested in trying his hot tea. Desperate to attract customers, he took a chance and added ice to the brew and was overwhelmed by the success of his newly-invented drink – iced tea.

Tea Innovations
In the early 1900s, an American travelling salesman, Thomas Sullivan, put small amounts of tea in silk drawstring bags so he could provide his customers with samples of his wares – and so the tea bag was born.

Tea Races and Tea-clippers

TRANSPORTING tea from China to London was a costly and time-consuming business and led to intense rivalry between ship owners, each eager to lead the field. The tea-clipper, a sleek, tall ship built for speed but large and strong enough to carry huge amounts of cargo, proved to be the early key to success, replacing the older frigate-built ships known jokingly as "tea-waggons". A clipper could reach speeds of up to 18 knots, even when it was carrying a typical tea cargo weighing approximately 454,000 kilograms (450 tons). In 1845 an

A nineteenth-century tea-clipper on the high seas.

American clipper smashed the 15-month journey time set by the East India Company and made the round trip from New York in less than eight months. Not to be beaten, the British built their own fleet of fast ships, including the most famous of all, the Cutty Sark. It is now in dry dock in Greenwich and can be visited.

Before long tea races became a popular sport, much to the delight of gamblers. In London bets were placed on the results of races, whilst the captain of the winning vessel stood to win a large bonus. The most celebrated tea race took place in mid-1866 when three of the forty competing vessels docked simultaneously in London, having made the journey from China in just 99 days.

The Chaa-sze

There was no mistaking the cargo of one particular British clipper, the Chaa-sze (Tea-taster), for it had a figurehead of a Chinese man and included representations of tea chests, teapots, cups and saucers.

The heyday of the tea-clipper was short lived. By 1870, the year after the Suez Canal was opened, they had been replaced by the revolutionary steamships which plied their way across the oceans, reducing the transport time by weeks.

Reading the Leaves

MANY people – especially those who could not afford a mote spoon (used for scooping loose leaf tea from the caddy to the teapot and skimming leaves from the surface of the tea once it had been poured into the cup) or a silver tea strainer – put great store in the power of the leaves which were left at the bottom of their cup, certain that when "read" they would reveal future events.

> *Matrons who toss the cup, and see*
> *The grounds of fate in grounds of tea.*

ALEXANDER POPE (N.D)

Postcard entitled *Stranger in the Teacup*.

The Power of the Leaves

Some pictures to look out for in the tea leaves at the bottom of your cup:

Anchor *A voyage*
Arrow *Bad news*
Bird *Good news or travel by air*
Cat *Good luck*
Circle *Trust and love*
Crescent moon *Changes*
Devil *Unbridled passions*
Dog *Good friends*
Door *An unusual event*
Eagle *Strength, overcoming adversity*
Egg *Increase*
Eye *Understanding*
Fairy *Romance*
Feather *Lack of concentration*
Fire *Impetuousness*
Fish *Fertility*
Flower *Happiness and success*
Geese *Sign of unwelcome visitors*
Heart *Love*
Iceberg *Hidden dangers*
Kite *Lofty ambitions*
Ladder *Advancement*
Mouth *Listen carefully*
Nest *Security*
Peacock *Immortality*
Pirate *Adventure*
Rainbow *Future good luck*
Ring *Marriage*
Sun *Warmth and happiness*
Tree *Recovery after an illness*
Vulture *Theft*

Tea and Health

DEVOTEES of tea never doubted that tea revived and refreshed and early advocates promoted it as a panacea for all ills, including headaches, weariness, colds, scurvy, dropsy and an unpleasant-sounding condition called "liptude distillations". In 1667 claims were made that tea was an effective treatment for gout. The first printed advertisement for tea appeared in 1669, by courtesy of Thomas Garway, the owner of the well-known London Coffee House, Garraways. He maintained that tea "would not only make the body active and lusty" but that it would "removeth the obstructions of the spleen". In recent years there has been much research into the health benefits of tea and many of the claims made hundreds of years ago have in fact been proved to be true.

Peter was not very well during the evening. His mother put him to bed, and made some chamomile tea: "One tablespoonful to be taken at bed-time."

PETER RABBIT *BEATRIX POTTER*

Tea Paraphernalia

TEA'S new found popularity was a blessing for entrepreneurs and craftsmen, for it created a huge industry of tea-related paraphernalia. From china to silver, linen to lace, everything that was produced reflected the fashions of the day.

One of the first people in Britain to take advantage of the manufacturing

Throughout the whole of England the drinking of tea is general. You have it twice a day and though the expense is considerable, the humblest peasant has his tea, just like the rich man.

LA ROUCHEFOUCAULD, 1784

opportunities was Josiah Wedgwood, a shrewd businessman and pioneering potter. In 1765 he was commissioned to make a tea and coffee service for Queen Charlotte, wife of the tea devotee King George III. The Queen was so delighted with this special cream ware set that she gave Royal Assent for Wedgwood to call the design "Queen's Ware".

Queen's Ware teapot and hot-water jug, circa 1765–70, showing traces of gilding in the moulding, most of which has been worn away.

Hot on Wedgwood's heels was Josiah Spode who, by 1815, had perfected the formula for making fine bone china. The brilliant whiteness and translucent beauty of Spode bone china so captivated the Prince of Wales that he later granted the company the first of their six royal

This section of a page from a 1900 Copeland catalogue shows the wide variety of cup shapes which were available to Victorian shoppers.

warrants. Europe had its own master craftsmen – factories at Meissen in Germany and Sèvres in France produced exquisite teasets that were hand-painted and often elaborately gilded.

Before long hostesses were demanding matching sets of tea-ware – not just the *de rigueur* teapot and mote spoon or tea strainer, but also a slop bowl to pour the dregs into, a sugar bowl with tongs, a milk jug and creamer and a teaspoon to stir with. Only later, during the Victorian era, did the tea cosy, cake-stand, bread and butter plate, tea knife, and cake and pastry forks become essential and fashionable items on the tea-table.

The ships that brought tea from China also carried tea-ware items, so it was not surprising that the Orient inspired the earliest European designs for teacups and saucers. But the Chinese practice of sipping hot tea from tea bowls – small cups without handles – was too much for the sensitive hands of British ladies. Manufacturers such as Spode and Wedgwood soon came up with a solution and created an innovative and more practical style of cup, which incorporated a handle, thus preventing delicate hands getting burnt.

However, tea was not always drunk from the cup. Saucers were added toward the end of the eighteenth century and were often used to cover the cup of tea while it infused. The tea was then poured into the saucer to be drunk.

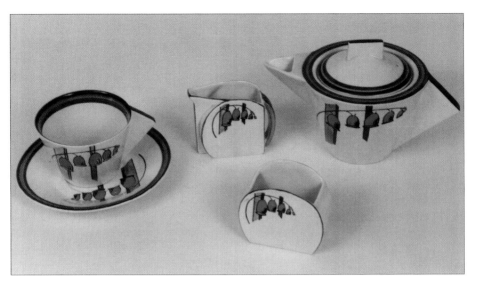

Part of the Bizarre ware collection, Solomon's Seal has a printed floral outline coloured in lilac, blue and green.

Fashions came and went and with them the shape of cups and handles changed. When Art Deco was the rage in the 1920s, Clarice Cliff (1899-1972), the celebrated English ceramic designer, created a range that was as unusual as its name. Made from earthenware, Bizarre's bold geometric design and continental shape captivated the public, only to be surpassed in popularity by Cliff's 1929 Conical Range with its solid triangular handles.

Too Hot to Handle
The Duchess of Lauderdale regretted her purchase of a set of silver teacups in 1672, for they were impossible to use as the handles became unbearably hot.

Teapots

...here was a table set out under a tree in front of the house, and the March Hare and the Hatter were having tea at it: ... the last time she saw them, they were trying to put the Dormouse into the teapot. "At any rate I'll never go there again!" said Alice...

ALICE'S ADVENTURES IN WONDERLAND
LEWIS CARROLL

THE first teapots to be imported into Europe from China were tiny, their size reflecting the high cost of tea. Wedgwood and Spode created delicate and highly decorated teapots whilst other manufacturers responded to current trends, producing novelty teapots in various shapes or caricatures of public figures. Silversmiths created tea-services that were both works of art, well suited to grace the homes of the rich and famous, and also items to be treasured as family heirlooms. Collecting was a fashion started by King George IV whilst he was the Prince Regent.

A magnificently worked Spode teapot in the Imari style with an abundance of gold, cobalt blue, emerald green and old scarlet from 1811. Pattern 1645.

The advent of electricity heralded a new adventure in tea-making. "Boiling the kettle" no longer meant having a kettle hanging over an open fire as the electric kettle became commonplace in the home. A more extraordinary invention for tea devotees was the automatic tea-maker, a machine that looked as if it would be more at home in one of W. Heath Robinson's comic illustrations.

The Tea Leaf

IMAGINE rolling hills in the tropics and sub-tropics and vast expanses of green shrubs, neatly pruned into level planes and one gets an idea of the plantations where the tea plant, *Thea Sinensis,* a member of the Camellia family, is grown. Altitude, temperature and rainfall are crucial elements in the tea-producing equation and each affects the quality of the end product. Even though there are more than 2,000 different varieties of tea, an experienced taster can identify the region, even the slope that a particular leaf was grown on and can detect how much rain fell the day the leaf was picked. In any one day a tea buyer may work their way through 400 samples, sipping it from a silver spoon to check, amongst other qualities, its "briskness" (how long the taste lingers in the mouth). The finest tea leaves are the young tender ones and in keeping with tradition, are generally still handpicked by women. The job is far from easy, particularly when one considers that the most superior leaves are grown at altitudes of 900–1,800 metres (3,000–6,000 feet) above sea-level. For the best results, freshly plucked leaves must be sent immediately for processing.

The tenderest top two leaves and bud are used in the highest grades of teas.

Growing tea bushes, following the natural contours of the lush landscape.

I pray thee, gentle Renny dear,
That thou will give to me,
With cream and sugar temper'd well,
Another dish of tea.

Nor fear that I, my gentle maid,
Shall long detain the cup,
When once unto the bottom I
Have drank the liquor up.

Yet hear, at last, this mournful truth,
Nor hear it with a frown,
Thou canst not make the tea so fast,
As I can gulp it down.

SAMUEL JOHNSON, TAKEN FROM
LIFE OF JOHNSON SIR JOHN HAWKINS

Types of Tea

THERE are six types of tea – black, green, white, oolong, scented and compressed.

Black tea includes Assam, Darjeeling and Nilgiri from India, Ceylon from Sri Lanka and Keemun and Lapsang Souchong from China – each of which has its own distinctive flavour and aroma. It is produced after the leaves have undergone four processing stages – withering (which happens when the leaves are laid out to dry), rolling, fermenting (a process which makes the leaves turn their familiar brownish colour and imparts a healthy flavour) and drying. Darjeeling – considered to be the champagne of teas – is grown at varying altitudes in the Himalayas and the higher up it is grown, the lighter the tea. Especially prized by connoisseurs is the new season's tea, the light and fragrant first flush Darjeeling, picked in April.

Oolong tea is semi-fermented and is generally the most expensive type of tea. The best varieties are produced in Taiwan and include the exclusive Monkey Picked.

Green tea, which is paler and milder than black tea, was the first to be enjoyed throughout the world, but its popularity waned as people showed a preference for a stronger brew. There are only two processing stages involved in producing green tea; rolling and drying. Varieties include Gunpowder from China and Matcha and Sencha from Japan.

White tea is produced in very small quantities in China and Sri Lanka and is available from specialist tea suppliers. A tea for the connoisseur.

Compressed teas are formed into ball, brick, nest and cake shapes. These are produced in China.

Scented teas are made from green, oolong or black teas flavoured with fruits, herbs, spices and flowers, such as roses, orchids and jasmine.

Blended teas have an important place in modern tea-drinking, particularly the English Breakfast tea blend. Originally a mix of black Indian and China teas, nowadays Assam, Ceylon and African teas are blended to provide drinkers with the three elements they require – strength, flavour and colour. More exotic sounding is Russian Caravan tea – named after the camel caravan that brought China tea to Europe along the silk and spice trade route – a blend of China tea. Earl Grey, so-called after Charles, Second Earl Grey who was the Prime Minister of Britain between 1830 and 1834, is a popular blend. Made with Indian and China teas, flavoured with bergamot oil, it is a refreshing tea, best served black or with lemon.

One Spoon or Two?

THE basic rules which most people follow today include using freshly drawn and boiled water and allowing one teaspoonful of loose leaf tea or one tea bag per person. Brewing time is, it is agreed, all-important and depends on the type of tea you are brewing. Darjeeling requires from 3 to 5 minutes, Kenya from 2 to 4 minutes and China Oolong 5 to 7 minutes. However, at what point you add milk has been a contentious subject for decades. Victorian

etiquette was definite on this matter: the milk or cream (a teaset always included a cream jug) had to be put in last, so that its addition could be rejected or limited. The British novelist and essayist, George Orwell (1903–1950), who published his own 11 golden rules for a "nice cup of tea" in 1945, had equally firm views. Last was best, he wrote, for "by putting the tea in first and then stirring as one pours, one can exactly regulate the amount of milk". The last word could go to Nancy Mitford, the English aristocrat novelist and biographer, who claimed that "milk in first", known as the "MIF" debate, was without doubt, not the "thing" to do.

Tea and Temperance

The domestic use of tea is a powerful champion able to encounter alcoholic drink in a fair field and throw it in a fair fight.

PRIME MINISTER GLADSTONE IN HIS BUDGET SPEECH OF 1882

PRIME Minister Gladstone was not the only Victorian to advocate tea-drinking, for the beverage was a boon to the Temperance Movement in their fight against the demon "drink". In cities like Liverpool, Birmingham and Preston, tea meetings were held which attracted as many as 2,500 people. Unsurprisingly, tea featured on the "menu" along with "singing, recitation and dialogue" – all intended to persuade folk to give up intoxicating liquor.

Tea Rationing

TEA has a reputation for being the national drink of Britain and at no time was its popularity greater than in wartime, when its restorative powers were so badly needed. It's hard to imagine now the effect that tea rationing had on a nation at war. But for 12 years, between 1940 and 1952, the government took charge of all tea imports, allocating it to dealers who then distributed it to shoppers. During this time the amount that each person was allowed per week varied between 50–75 grammes (2–2½ ounces) and there must have been a great sigh of relief in homes up and down the land when rationing finally came to an end in 1952.

Punch magazine captured the British weakness for tea in this wartime cartoon, entitled *War Time Weaknesses – Cups of Tea.*

A cup of tea was welcomed by these two youngsters who were evacuated from London in June 1940. It made them feel at home in strange surroundings.

—— *Outdoor and Travelling Tea* ——

Since the early eighteenth century, tea has been a favourite drink to be enjoyed in all situations – tea gardens and parties, picnic teas and travelling teas.

Tea Gardens

THERE were more than 500 coffee houses selling tea by 1700, but by 1730 these all-male establishments had fallen out of favour and become the haunts of scoundrels and villains. High society – which included ladies – had now found a more salubrious way of enjoying afternoon tea in the new tea gardens which had sprung up, especially in the metropolis.

Between 1732 and about 1852, tea gardens including Vauxhall in South London, Marylebone, Ranelagh in Chelsea and Bagnigge Wells, east of London's Grays Inn Road, were the places where fashionable Georgians went to see and be seen. At Ranelagh they could expect to be served with "fine Imperial tea and other delicious refreshments" whilst at Vauxhall they could enjoy the beauty of a most enchanting lily garden.

> 66 *Old Vauxhall Gardens must have been a charming place for flirtations, for the windings and turnings in the wildernesses were so intricate that the most experienced mothers often lost themselves in looking for their daughters.* 99
>
> **HIGHWAYS AND BYWAYS IN LONDON,**
> *E. COOK (1902)*

Bagnigge Wells Tea Garden in 1778. The centre of the garden had a small round fishpond, in the midst of which was a curious fountain representing a Cupid astride a swan. Water spouted out of the swan's beak at a great height, much to the delight of onlookers.

Harmony and music were the great traditions of the Marylebone Tea Garden and the composer Handel regularly visited to listen to his cantatas being performed. A less welcome visitor was the burly Duke of Cumberland (1721–1765) who was renowned for disturbing the peaceful atmosphere by his rude behaviour. Bagnigge Wells was regarded by the ladies as "the last word of modish resort". A contemporary writer described the gardens: "... laid out with clipped hedges of yew, the formal walks edged by box and holly and the arbours covered with sweetbrier and honeysuckle for tea drinking".

At night the walkways of the tea gardens were illuminated by lanterns, transforming the ornately landscaped gardens into entrancing, magical places. Ordinary folk soon adopted the tea garden idea and more modest venues opened up, offering the working classes, who were thrilled at the opportunity of a day out, a value-for-money excursion.

Visitors of all classes could spend their time watching events from the shelter of stylish, well-furnished arbours and the entertainment – musicians, fireworks, acrobats, jugglers and magicians – was lavish. The entrance fee, which always included the unlimited "regale" of tea, coffee and bread and butter, varied from place to place and time of day. An entirely different type of tea garden had emerged by the 1930s, in locations such as Kew Gardens and Hyde Park. Here visitors could enjoy a pot of tea at a table under an umbrella for less than half the price charged at the grander tea gardens.

Tea-garden Parties

FROM the moment that Queen Victoria held her first royal tea party at Buckingham Palace in 1868, the idea of the tea-garden party became a popular, fashionable and very English entertainment. The royal connection enhanced the reputation of

Photographed in 1951 in the grounds of Buckingham Palace, Queen Elizabeth, the Queen Mother was fond of the Nippys, who regularly served at her London garden parties. On this occasion the Nippys were not wearing their starched white coronet caps – perhaps they didn't want to be seen to be competing with royalty.

Ridgway's, the tea importers, for they were invited to create a special blend for Queen Victoria. This blend was then served at garden parties, alongside the finger sandwiches and pastries. Just how regular the royal garden parties were before 1948 is difficult to say, but between 1948 and 1958 the monarch was "at home" in London to specially invited guests on two afternoons in July – and on one such occasion whilst in summer residence at the Palace of Holyrood House, in Edinburgh. Garden parties are still a regular event at Buckingham Palace. For many years J. Lyons and Co. were the official caterers and the famous Nippy waitress was to be seen on the lawns of Buckingham Palace (see page 40).

Afternoon Tea

UP until the 1840s tea was only drunk at breakfast or after dinner as a digestif, but once again the aristocracy played its part in changing fashion. For it was Anna Maria, the Seventh Duchess of Bedford, who is popularly credited with introducing the idea of afternoon tea. By all accounts she suffered from such gnawing hunger pains in the long gap between lunch and dinner at 9 o'clock, that she ordered her maid to serve tea and cakes at 5 o'clock to alleviate these "sinking feelings". This was the start of the formal afternoon tea.

The Tea Break and High Tea

A different gap was filled by the tea break which was introduced more than 200 years ago. Labourers and rural workers were served tea and food mid-morning and late afternoon to tide them over until they returned home for their evening meal. For many workers, afternoon tea was replaced by high tea, an end-of-working-day meal which combined tea and early supper. This tradition still lingers on, particularly in the north of England and Scotland. Hearty hot and cold food is served alongside cakes, bread, butter and jam and the not-to-be forgotten pot of steaming tea, with all its restorative powers.

These London and North Eastern Railway workers are being served tea by a tealady in the workshops at Temple Mills, watched closely by their supervisor. This photograph was taken in July 1941.

Tea Picnics

WITH the public taste for taking tea out-of-doors well established, a new idea, that of the tea picnic, evolved. Victorian and Edwardian society were particularly partial to these outings, so much so that Mrs Beeton (1836–65), the Victorian authority on cookery and domestic science, whose

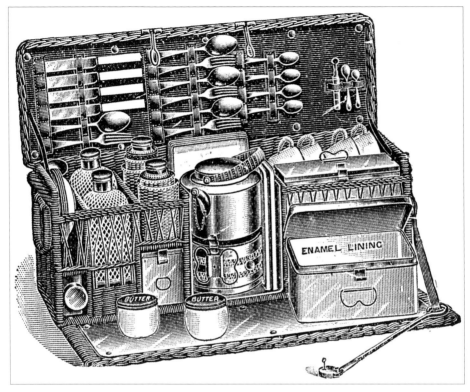

This tea basket was one of a dozen or more designs available to the discerning Harrods shopper in 1912.

renowned *Book on Household Management* was first published in 1861, included picnic menus in her publications. Tea was clearly an essential part of the ritual, for she advised that "A kettle and teapot must be taken if they cannot be borrowed; nor should a box of matches, a little dry wood and a cloth for wiping cups be forgotten". Society events and the "season", which included horse-racing at Ascot and Epsom, boating at Henley Royal Regatta, cricket at Lord's, opera at Glyndbourne and tennis at Wimbledon, provided followers of fashion with the ideal opportunity of enjoying a lavish tea picnic.

In fact it seems that visitors often took more interest in the traditional serving of tea than the event itself. Tables and chairs would be set out with crisp, fresh linen cloths and neatly folded napkins and the full range of tea-ware – including silver teapot and hot-water jug – would appear. There was no problem in safely transporting all the paraphernalia because specially designed tea-picnic baskets had been introduced by the most renowned department stores, for just such occasions. The invention of the Thermos flask in 1904 enabled Edwardian travellers to keep their drinks piping hot.

However you travelled there was always a cup of tea around the corner, as these cyclists in Cotesbach, Leicestershire discovered in 1935.

Travelling Tea

TEA was such an important part of everyday life for the Victorians that it rapidly became available wherever they went. This was the golden age of the railways and the train companies quickly saw the potential for extra profit by satisfying the thirsty passengers. The first railway buffet to serve tea was opened by the catering company, Spiers and Pond, on Farringdon Station, London, in 1866. The fully-equipped tea trolley – including the near-indestructible aspidistra plant, so beloved of the Victorians – made its first appearance on the platforms of main-line stations and liveried staff served a wide selection of refreshments to waiting passengers.

Alternatively, travellers could purchase a specially-fitted tea basket to take with them on their journey. Day or night, staff were on hand when trains arrived at stations, ready to deliver the complete kit. The Great Western Railways basket had an enamelled-iron lining and contained hot water, milk, sugar, three slices of bread and butter, cake and a piece of fresh fruit.

First-class passengers could, if they preferred, have afternoon tea served on board the train. In the comfort of their private compartment, perhaps on their way to connect with an Atlantic liner docked in Liverpool, a Victorian lady would partake of toasted teacakes, assorted sandwiches and cakes, alongside the pot of Indian or

China tea. But, as the Great Western Railway were to discover years later, the cost of serving cups of tea on the trains was unexpectedly expensive. For just before the outbreak of the Second World War, the company reported that they lost an astonishing 240,000 of their specially stamped cups every year. Some certainly turned up in the soldier's kit, but where the rest went to remains a mystery.

When the motorcar became the latest mode of travel, drivers and their entourage had no difficulty in obtaining a cup of tea during their journey, especially in the south of England. Apart from the roadside café, the 1930s holidaymaker could rely upon the tea caravan – a caravan drawn by a small motorcar – which was located at popular roadside spots, serving holidaymakers with tea and cakes.

Imagine the thrill for the really adventurous tea-loving traveller, when in 1927, during the months of May to October, the Imperial Airways Company ran regular afternoon flights over the City of London and served a first class tea.

The aircraft used for the afternoon flights over the City of London was the Armstrong Whitworth Argosy. Passengers would get a wonderful view of the metropolis whilst...

Tea at the Cinema

No afternoon visit to the cinema in the 1930s and 1940s was complete without a cup of tea. Patrons could order a tray of tea to be brought to them in their seats during the intermission. If you visited one of the "super" cinemas – one of the larger, more elaborate venues which sprang up everywhere after 1929 – you could enjoy a pot of the beverage in the cinema café, to the accompaniment of a Palm Court orchestra.

...drinking their tea and sampling delicious food in less-than-spacious conditions.

── Tea and Symphony ──

This is the story of how dancing and afternoon tea combined to become a fashionable and popular form of entertainment and how the tango started it all.

Tea-dancing

> *What could be pleasanter, for instance,*
> *on a dull wintry afternoon,*
> *at five o'clock or so, when calls or shopping*
> *are over, than to drop in*
> *to one of the cheery little "Thé Dansant"*
> *clubs, which have sprung up*
> *all over the West End…to take one's place*
> *at a tiny table…to enjoy a*
> *most elaborate and delicious tea…whilst*
> *listening to an excellent string*
> *band (and)…joining in the dance…*

MRS GLADYS CROZIER, 1913

WHEN Mrs Gladys Crozier, society hostess and leading authority on tea-dancing, wrote these words in her authoritative book on the subject in 1913, little did she know how popular this form of entertainment would become. Some of London's elite had toyed with the idea of a "dancing" tea in 1845, much to the amusement of the recently launched, humorous satirical journal *Punch*. On the other hand, continental society was already well accustomed to the afternoon diversion, for fashionable Moroccans regularly danced a gentle valse around the afternoon tea-table. Similarly tea-dancing had already caught on in the best Parisian drawing-rooms. But,

what started out as a respectable, harmless diversion in France, was soon transformed into a daring and risqué spectacle, all due to the arrival of the very provocative Argentine tango on French dance floors around 1912.

The Origins of Tango
Gladys Crozier gave two explanations for the word "tango". One said it was derived from tangonette, *the name of a special kind of castanet, the other from the verb* tangir, *to touch.*
(The Times Literary Supplement, *18 December 1913)*

Suddenly "tango teas" became the rage of high society. The high-class dress-designer Lady Duff Gordon – otherwise known by her professional name of Madame Lucile – recalled how everyone in Paris was "tango-mad" before the First World War, "from *la haute société* down to the little *midinettes* who could be seen practising new steps in the Jardin des Tuileries in their lunch-hour." Parisians, who were known to be daring and trend-setting, had never seen anything to compare with the sensuous

An amusing satirical view of the tea dance entitled *Thé Dansante*, in an 1845 edition of *Punch*, which had more to do with balancing skills than dancing talent.

tango. Nor had Kaiser Wilhelm of Germany, who had banned the dance because he thought it totally decadent and only Bohemian café society in Argentina dared to dance it. From capital to coast, the tango tea became the most popular pastime amongst high society. Sophisticated socialites in the fashionable resorts of Deauville and Dinard were guaranteed an afternoon's tango tea at the casino or any of the best hotels. In Lucerne, the elite establishments vied for clients to tango at teatime; and not to be left out, the dance got Ostend "...by the throat". Returning to British shores, the dance crossed the high seas and by 1913 tango teas were making headline news in London and being advertised in many of the popular papers.

> ### Tango Lessons
> *Fortunes were made from dancing lessons in Paris. In 1913,* The Daily Mail *reported that a Parisian instructor was working from breakfast-time to late in the evening, giving half-hour long tango classes to groups of two or three pupils in the Place Vendome, and charging each person £12. Put into context; in Britain in 1912, the average annual income was £80.*

Tango teas at the Prince's Restaurant in Piccadilly were one of the social highlights of late 1913. Every day a wide central space was cleared and all the tables gathered around so that guests had a bird's eye view of the professional dancing demonstration.

The Place to be Seen

LIKE the rush for tea-ware a century before, "tangomania" led to an explosion of golden opportunities for entrepreneurs. From people hurrying to open tea-dance clubs, to dressmakers, milliners and cobblers frantically trying to produce suitable dresses, hats and shoes, to teachers vying to give lessons, the atmosphere was quite feverish in Edwardian London. Amongst the most enthusiastic were the new generation of tea-dancers, who suddenly found themselves freed from the strict constraints of Victorian society. After all, what danger could there be in young men and women meeting, unchaperoned, in public in the afternoon, to share the pleasure of a cup of tea and a dance?

Amongst the most select tea-dance clubs to open in the metropolis were the "Four Hundred Club" in Old Bond Street, the Carlton Hotel, the Thé Tango Club at Prince's Restaurant and the Boston Club at the Grafton Gallery. The "Four Hundred Club" included "Royalty, an English Duke or two, many well-known peers and some of the most shining lights of the musical-comedy stage" amongst its members.

But of all the tea-dance venues in London, there was nowhere that could compare with the Savoy. The tea-dance experience at the Savoy was the ultimate in good taste, style and sophistication. The tea-tables were beautifully set with the hotel's hallmark pink tablecloths, *le thé Russe* was prepared by a Russian expert and menus were presented in French to preserve the continental feel so loved by high society. A magnificent new rising ballroom floor was installed in the restaurant foyer in 1928, much to the chagrin of their envious competitors. Patrons enjoying a tango tea at the Savoy in the 1920s were serenaded by the first genuine tango band to play in the country. And in November 1933, teatime visitors were the first to see a new dance, the Charleston Blues, demonstrated on the Savoy dance floor by the champion ballroom dancer, Victor Silvester.

These charming *thé dansant* menus set the scene for a totally indulgent afternoon tea at The Savoy.

As the tango craze gained momentum, expert tuition became a must and many teachers combined lessons with a tea dance. A Miss Lennard was in attendance at the select tea dance at the Waldorf Hotel, whilst Miss Belle Harding, presided over *thé tangos* at the Hotel Cecil and the Royal Palace Hotel Kensington – that was when she was not gallivanting around organizing *thé dansant* and tango teas the length and breadth of the country. These out-of-town events were so popular that hundreds of would-be dancers were apparently turned away from venues each week.

Even though the tango was modified to make it more acceptable and respectable, many Edwardians expressed outrage and the popular press was littered with anti-tango letters denouncing the dance as "indecent, scandalous and obscene".

Maurice and Leonora Hughes were the exhibition dancers at this *thé dansant* held in the restaurant foyer of the Savoy Hotel in October 1920. The band playing that day were Sherbo's Orchestra, a five-piece American band.

As letters in the papers from amateur social reformers would have us imagine it.

And as we have actually seen it.

This cartoon, *The Tango in the Ball-room* appeared in *Punch* in December of 1913.

Frocks Galore

THE fashion for afternoon tea breathed new life into late-Victorian and Edwardian dress design, for the tight-waisted and bustled dresses of the day left little room for sandwiches and cakes, however dainty they were. By the 1880s, the Dress Reform Society were already encouraging women to wear less restrictive and harmful clothing and a more relaxed style of garment began to emerge, much to the delight of the couture dressmaker. To be thoroughly fashionable the hostess who was entertaining at home wore one of the new tea gowns – a loose and luxurious creation of velvet and silk which was feminine but

still refined. Dressing for the *thé dansant*, however, called for an altogether more elaborate garment and one that would allow for freedom of movement – a very novel idea indeed.

One of Mrs Crozier's favourite designers was Madame Lucile. Each of her delicious tango-tea frocks was given a tantalizing title – such as "You'd better ask me" and "Carnival" and were worn by the rich and famous. Fabulously luxurious fabrics like chiffon, velvet, net and fur were combined with superb artistry to create beautiful, feminine frocks.

These dresses were the creation of Messrs Boué Soeurs of the Rue de la Paix, Paris and Conduit Street, London. Glorious garments of satin draped over chiffon velours, silk and sable, black and rose shot taffetas – adorned by chenille embroidery and scalloped edges with velvet trim.

The less well-heeled could rely upon the classic little black dress with its obligatory draped skirt, whilst those who were handy with a needle and thread could make a dainty dress using one of the simple patterns featured in the well-known ladies' magazine, *Queen*. As a last resort "ordinary outdoor calling and shopping clothes" could be worn. The accoutrements that went with the London *thé dansant* outfit included an "ultra piquant" hat, possibly in black velvet adorned by an ostrich feather, black shoes and the finest of black silk stockings.

Not to be outdone, men became equally fashion-conscious and the smartest of them appeared at the *thé dansant* wearing a black morning coat, waistcoat, pin-striped trousers and black boots.

The First World War and After

THE outbreak of the First World War in 1914 put a damper on the well-established big social dances. Officers were officially forbidden to dance in uniform and even though tea dances were an excellent form of relaxation for men on a few days leave,

they had to look elsewhere for their entertainment. But once the war was over tea dances rapidly reappeared on the social scene throughout the country. Besides the established clubs and hotels that opened again for business, department stores jumped on the bandwagon. In May 1919 William Whiteley's department store in Queensway, London, started holding tea dances every afternoon in their new restaurant. In Paris, theatres and music halls were converted into dancing halls, specializing in tango teas.

By 1926, there were so many tea-dance venues to choose from in London that if you were fortunate and money was no object, it was possible to tango every afternoon of the week. Costs varied tremendously depending on the venue – the Italian Roof Garden at the Criterion, with its ethereal décor, was twice as expensive as the Regent Palace Hotel. The Café de Paris and the Café Verrey in Regent Street vied for custom with Lyons Popular Café in

Before the Hammersmith Palais de Dance opened in 1919, London had never had a big dance hall. It had a good floor, a colour scheme of lights and decorative effects, continuous music and many tables for tea and talk.

Piccadilly, the Trocadero and the Georgian Restaurant at Harrods department store. Londoners seemed to have an insatiable appetite for tea-dancing and flocked to the new *palais de dance* which sprang up around the capital, offering thousands of ordinary people the chance of dancing at teatime as well as in the evenings. The Hammersmith Palais de Dance, which opened its doors in October 1919, could accommodate 2,500 people and was described as "the largest and most luxurious dancing palace in Europe". The maple wood dance floor was so valuable that dancers had to exchange their own shoes for special dance slippers. The number of boots and shoes that were left behind after the dancing was over amazed the proprietors.

Now that you've learnt to dance
That new Brazilian prance
Go on and show them all you know
Dance it to and fro, Do it nice and slow.
Now for your partner reach,
And do the new Mattchiche
It's Tango Tea-time when that
melody starts.

COME WITH ME TO THE TANGO TEA,
WORDS BY CON CONRAD (**STAR,** 1913)

The Locarno Ballroom, established in 1929, boasted the only revolving bandstand in the country. Elsewhere, the tea dance became a regular feature at holiday camps, whilst those cruising on the high seas enjoyed less formal tea dances.

The popularity of "taxi boys" (professional dancing partners) increased every year in the cafés of Montparnasse, Paris. This group were waiting for partners who would pay 1 franc 50 centimes for a dance.

To Tango or Turkey Trot?

DANCE crazes came and went on the tea-dance floor: from the tango to the turkey-trot; the shimmy to the shake; the bunny hug to the black bottom and the castle walk. Another popular dance, the Lindy hop, was named after Charles Lindbergh, the American pilot who made the first solo crossing of the Atlantic in June 1927.

One of the most energetic but potentially hazardous dances was the Charleston. The first demonstration was given at a special *thé dansant* at the Carnival Club in London in 1925, to riotous results. The flapping of legs, kicking of heels and waving of arms caused so many injuries that shortly after an extraordinary notice began to appear in the dancehalls. Patrons were implored to "Please Charleston Quietly", displayed as "P. C. Q." in many dancehalls, to try and minimize injuries.

The Second World War

IT was a sad day when, in 1936, The Savoy stopped holding *thés dansants*. But eager tango dancers were still being catered for around the corner at the Waldorf Hotel, which had been holding regular tea dances

Apart from the draw of big name bands – Stroud Hoxton, Art Hickman's Fives, Harry Pilcer and Murray's Savoy Quartette – mannequin parades and exhibition dancers were added attractions at many tea dances. Professional dancing partners – never referred to as gigolos – were provided as part of the service at The Savoy but bore little resemblance to the brilliantined and button-holed "taxi boys" whom French mademoiselles could hire at the cafés of Montparnasse, Paris for a dance.

in their magnificent Palm Court restaurant since the early 1920s. The strains of Mr Mantovani's famed orchestra were heard there until the outbreak of the Second World War in September 1939.

Dancehalls and cinemas closed immediately as the blackout and threat of night raids affected evening events. But a nation at war craved amusement and informal relaxation more than ever and as the afternoon was a relatively safe time of day, tea dances continued to flourish. Huge teatime crowds clamouring for a diversion overwhelmed reopened venues. Now "swing" and "jitterbug" – imported from America – were the dances of the day. Wartime rations meant that more modest food was served and the cucumber finger

sandwiches and French fancies were replaced by frugal picnics. In peacetime, with holidays once more on the family agenda, visitors to the immensely popular Butlin's camps at Skegness and Clacton, enjoyed the regular tea dances.

Tea-dancing at the Turn of the Twenty-first Century

WHO would have thought that tea-dancing would, in a post modern era, still draw the crowds? But nostalgia and the pull of leisurely pastimes have ensured the survival, even revival, of what is essentially a most pleasurable entertainment. The early decades of the 1900s may have been the heyday of the tea dance, but now, as then, there are all sorts of venues up and down the country where you can take tea and tango. At one end of the spectrum there is a community hall in South Wales where the dance music is played on a magnificent "Christie" Wurlitzer organ, rescued from a 1930s cinema and where the tea is made by local ladies. On the other hand you could splash out and take a trip down memory lane by attending one of the weekend tea dances held regularly at The Savoy hotel in London and in the Floral Hall at the Royal Opera House, Covent Garden. You'll be enraptured by the style and sense of occasion which have lost nothing in the passage of time. As the dances are as popular as ever, would-be tango dancers must book a table in advance and, whilst the cost has inevitably increased since 1928, little else has changed.

Tearooms and Teashops

There are many intriguing stories behind the growth in popularity of the tearoom – including the Temperance movement, the Victorian addiction to shopping and the J. Lyons Nippy waitress.

Pioneering Scots

> *There's a cozy tea room dear,*
> *Not so very far from here,*
> *Where no one else can find us,*
> *There we'll go and leave the world*
> *behind us…*
>
> 1923 SONG

BY the middle of the nineteenth century Victorian society, rich and poor, had a real taste for afternoon tea. Whether it was a tea for two, a gossipy tea, a ladies-only tea or a "respite before returning home from work tea," people wanted to enjoy this new pleasure and to do so away from their homes. Glaswegians were the luckiest for they were the first to be introduced to the delights of the tearoom. It was in Glasgow in 1875 that an enterprising and adventurous young tea dealer, Mr Stuart Cranston, pioneered the idea of such an establishment. Temperance and the idea that tea was "the cup which cheers but not inebriates" certainly influenced Mr Cranston, for he had strong family connections with the movement and an eye for business and saw that working people needed somewhere to refresh themselves during the day. He was a canny Scot who noticed that leisured ladies, who had taken

to shopping as a full-time hobby, craved a place to take the weight off their tired feet during spending sprees. For, up until the appearance of the tearoom and shop, there was nowhere a Victorian lady could have a meal on her own and nowhere she could respectably meet her friends outside of the home.

Shopping was certainly important to the Victorians, but having tea was even more important, as this satirical cartoon from 1893 shows so amusingly.

Cranston's success set a new trend north of the border and by 1901 there were so many tearooms in Glasgow that the city was described as "a very Tokio for tearooms". But the most famous and distinctive venue was yet to make its debut. When Miss Cranston, Stuart's sister, opened her famous Willow Tea Rooms on fashionable Sauchiehall Street in November 1903 – she already had a small empire of

The front tearoom at The Willow showing the strange series of plaster relief panels set in a frieze. The table is set for tea.

artistic tearooms – Glaswegians were overwhelmed by its splendour. The art nouveau style was the very epitome of chic, a veritable *tour de force* of Miss Cranston's partnership with the unconventional architect, designer and artist Charles Rennie Mackintosh (1868–1928) and it set tongues wagging for months. The young architect, Edward Lutyens, was almost lost for words – and possibly a little jealous – when he described the design as "gorgeous, a wee bit vulgar…it is all quite good, all just a little *outré*", or as we would say now "over-the-top".

Refreshment in London

MEANWHILE, south of the border, there were few places that working or shopping Londoners could go for refreshment, other than the public houses where no self-respecting female would be seen. That is until 1880, when the resourceful manageress of the London Bridge branch of the Aerated Bread Company (ABC) persuaded her employers to open up a public tearoom at the back of the store. The venture proved to be as popular with ladies of high society as with shop assistants, typists and ordinary shoppers and very quickly the idea was being copied across the metropolis.

Of all the teashops to open, those belonging to J. Lyons & Co. Ltd. were undoubtedly the most popular and enduring. The very first branch opened its doors in London in 1894 at 213 Piccadilly and was an immediate success. The design was meant to stun and the French influence ensured this: the walls were lined with silk damask, the tables topped with marble and the chairs upholstered with red plush – a truly splendid place to enjoy afternoon tea and pastries. With 17 teashops to their name by 1898, the owners adopted a new "house style" and subsequent branches were resplendent with opal glass ceiling panels and walls lined in marble. Only the bentwood chairs hinted at practicality. J. Lyons & Co. Ltd. strove constantly to appeal to the widest audience and their "Popular Café", the first of which opened in London in 1904, was a testimony to this commitment. Who could fail to be attracted to a teashop which was an extravaganza of Edwardian opulence and gilt richness and which promised to provide "luxury for the millions"? Clearly not the hundreds of customers, many of them lady shoppers, who were enticed to "afternoon tea between 3 and 6" and tempted with "delicious new pastries at 2d, tea at 3d per pot and no gratuities".

Lyons continued to prosper and in 1910 a new branch was being opened approximately every two weeks. Besides London, cities including Bradford, Liverpool, Manchester and Bristol all had

The actress Binnie Hale on the cover of *Lyons Mail* in November 1930. She played the heroine in the musical comedy *Nippy*.

their Lyons teashop, as well as their Nippy waitresses. Indeed the company owed much of its success to these extraordinary ladies. In the beginning Lyons' waitresses were called "Gladys", but the name "Nippy" – very apt given the way they went about their job – was adopted following a

Nippy School
The Nippy School of Instruction was set up in 1912 by Nell Bacon, one of the very first Lyons' waitresses. She was convinced that if she had been properly trained in the 1890s, she would not have ended up emptying a cup of tea into the upturned top-hat of one of her gentlemen customers.

company competition in 1924. By then the Nippy training school had been running for 12 years, preening young women for what was considered a prestigious job. Efficient and smart, the Nippy – a great British institution in her own right – enchanted all her customers, from the royalty she served at Buckingham Palace garden parties to the humblest customer in the teashop. Wearing a black dress, starched apron, white collar, cuffs and cap, the Lyons waitress could always be relied upon to give service with a smile – and the most successful member of staff could become a "Star" Nippy and win the coveted annual prize of £100.

Tea in Paris

The Englishman abroad in Paris at the turn of the twentieth century had to look no further than the Rue de Rivoli for his cup of tea. For when the stationers, W. H. Smith, opened their first branch there in 1903, they provided customers with a tearoom where "real English tea and buns could be drunk and eaten."

A Suitable Job

A multitude of new tearooms and shops opened in London, many of them owned and managed by women, for this seemed, at the time, to be a very suitable occupation for the fairer sex. Not everyone

agreed and one expert on the subject warned, in 1902, that running a teashop was "not such a profitable business as aspiring lady teashop owners might imagine." This gloomy prospect did little to deter the pioneering women of the day, who located their establishments in the most expensive – and most prestigious – streets of London. Despite the cost of rent in fashionable Bond Street, in 1893, the Ladies' Own Tea Association opened here. This enchanting establishment was noted in the press for its dainty interior. Others soon followed suit, including The Kettledrum Tea Rooms, owned by Miss Cohen. Undaunted by any words of caution, she moved her already much-talked-about and thriving business to Old Bond Street in 1896. The charming pink and primrose décor appealed to lady shoppers and only those with strong willpower could resist the tempting delicacies produced by Messrs. Fuller, the American confectioners – renowned for their delectable iced walnut cake. The Fullers' shop, which opened in Kensington High Street in 1892, was described as "the prettiest shop in the world – all alcoves, palms and delightful décor with little tables spread for tea, which ladies will find a perfect boon".

Another venue, the Studio Tea Rooms, which started business in 1897, offered a different ambience – that of a drawing-room rather than a shop – for it was established to serve "visitors from the country and other ladies who could not afford the luxury of a club".

Tea and Shopping

BY the mid-1880s customers in the fashionable department stores had good reason to linger, for many of these emporiums boasted their own tearooms – Whiteley's, Swan and Edgar, Derry and Toms, to name but a few. Harrods Grand Restaurant and, from 1911, their Rock Tea Gardens – situated on the roof terrace and with décor that was reminiscent of a Mediterranean garden – were amongst the recognized social rendezvous, probably the most prestigious in town. Their patrons were served tea to the melodic strains of Harrods' Royal Red Orchestra.

Further north, in Manchester, Messrs. Kendal Milne opened a tearoom in 1890, extravagantly decorated in the Moorish style, but this was not as sumptuous and mystical as Liberty's Arab Tea Room, located on the first floor of the smart Regent Street store in London. Besides serving tea in Eastern surroundings, it sold Indian condiments and, amazingly for the time, offered female visitors the ultimate convenience – a ladies' cloakroom. Sauchiehall Street in Glasgow had Pettigrew and Stephens, whose generous practice of complimentary tea for their customers ended in 1898, when a moderate charge was introduced "to remove all idea of indebtedness from the minds of patrons".

Harrods Grand Restaurant in 1909, when it featured the Royal Red Orchestra during afternoon tea.

This delightful, early 1930s tea pavilion, in the heart of Kensington Gardens, was designed by the architect J. Grey West and replaced an older decrepit building.

Popularity of Tea

As long as tea was popular the tearoom remained a firm favourite. The big names in tea like Ridgway's, Liptons and, of course, Lyons, had their venues on the high street, firmly in the public eye, but many suffered damage during the Second World War. Lyons knew that the morale boosting powers of tea were especially needed during wartime and quickly set up emergency teashops wherever there was an area of distress. A specially built Lyons commercial vehicle would tow a trailer van in camouflage, from which the public and members of the emergency services were served with free tea and buns, day and night. A truly patriotic gesture which was much appreciated by all. The last surviving Lyons teashop closed in January 1981.

Less noticeable than the high street teashop was the traditional tea pavilion, like the one in Kensington Gardens, which was rebuilt in 1934. Today, visitors to the East Gallery of the Serpentine Gallery would never suspect that this was once a very popular tea place.

Up and down the country there are venues where the tradition of afternoon tea not only survives, but thrives. The traditional fare of delicate finger sandwiches, scones with fresh cream and jam, delicate cakes and pastries and a pot of tea is still served, whether in the grand setting of a city hotel or in a small, traditional country tearoom. Fashions come and go but the British love of tea remains undiminished for the beverage has a special place in the hearts and minds of millions of people. Given the exciting and often curious history of tea, I have no doubt that it will remain as popular for centuries to come.

—Where To— Take Tea

Taking afternoon tea is an extremely civilized way of passing a pleasant couple of hours with friends whilst enjoying delicious food and a refreshing cup of tea. It also offers you the chance to be part of a tradition that has been popular in Britain for over 100 years.

How to Use This Guide

CHOOSING tea places to include has been a difficult task for there were many more which could have been mentioned. Those selected all serve an excellent traditional afternoon tea in the most congenial of surroundings and you can be sure of a warm welcome wherever you go. Some are more formal than others, but none are pretentious. I have included a range of places, from small family-run farms to exclusive hotels, museum cafés to Victorian tearooms. Many of them are in central locations, close to major tourist attractions and centres but some require just a little more effort to find.

This section is divided into two directories, the first guiding you to some of the very best places to take tea in London (see pages 47–69) and the second pointing you towards more than 25 places outside of London in England, Scotland and Wales (see pages 70–95). The entries in the London directory are listed A–Z by the name of the establishment. The second directory, "Rest of Britain" has been divided alphabetically by country, county and place name. There is also a directory listing on the opening page of each section so that you can easily find the place that you want.

Each entry starts with the full name of the establishment, where tea is taken, the address, telephone and fax numbers, e-mail and website addresses, followed by details of opening hours and when afternoon tea is served, basic menu information, whether or not smoking is permitted, public transport or location details, advice on where to park and some ideas of other places in the area that you may like to visit. This information is followed by a description of the venue and the afternoon tea.

All of the places listed have disabled access and welcome children unless otherwise stated. However, it is best to telephone ahead of your visit if you have any particular requirements. Most of the places listed will cater for those with special dietary requirements but appreciate advance notice, so again it is wise to ring prior to your visit to check that your particular needs can be met.

Each place has been allocated either one, two or three teacup symbols. I want to stress that this is not an indication of quality, but a quick reference guide as to the atmosphere of the place and the kind of experience that you can expect to have when taking tea there.

> ☕ Afternoon tea in a relaxed setting.
> ☕☕ A slightly more formal experience.
> ☕☕☕ Tea in grand surroundings.

London

THE BRITISH MUSEUM

Court Restaurant
Great Russell Street, London WC1B 3DG
Tel 020 7323 8990 (for tea reservations;
booking recommended)
Fax 020 7323 8979
e-mail britishmuseum@digbytrout.co.uk
www.digbytrout.co.uk

Afternoon tea 3.30–5.00pm
Monday–Wednesday; 3.30–9.00pm
Thursday–Saturday; 3.30–6.00pm Sunday
Three set teas or tea à la carte
No smoking
Nearest underground stations Russell
Square, Tottenham Court Road, Holborn
Parking Public car parks in Bloomsbury
Square and Southampton Row; meter
parking
Places of interest nearby Covent Garden,
Sir John Soame Museum, Bloomsbury

Those of us, like myself, who were regular
users of the Round Reading Room at the
British Library, cannot cease to be amazed
by Norman Foster's spectacular
transformation of the space which is now
the Great Court – the largest covered
courtyard in Europe. Taking afternoon tea
on the sixth floor, under the glass roof and
with views overlooking the Great Court, is
an awesome experience and one not to be
missed. Choose a traditional afternoon tea
of fruit scone, clotted cream and jam, and a
slice of cake from the day's home-made
selection. Add sandwiches – smoked
salmon as well as cream cheese and

cucumber – to this if you are feeling
hungry and for a touch of luxury include a
glass of champagne. Teas on offer (bagged
only) include Assam, English Breakfast,
Darjeeling, Earl Grey and four fruit
varieties. Children are very welcome, with
high chairs, complimentary baby food and
colouring books provided on request.
When you have finished your tea, don't
miss the opportunity of visiting one of the
world's great library rooms which was a
popular refuge for literary luminaries
including Karl Marx, Virginia Woolf,
Rudyard Kipling and Oscar Wilde.

RAFFLES BROWN'S HOTEL

The Drawing Room
33–34 Albemarle Street, London W1S 4BP
Tel 020 7518 4108 (for tea reservations;
weekday bookings only, weekends are "first
come, first served")
Fax 020 7493 9381
e-mail tea@brownshotel.com
www.brownshotel.com

Afternoon tea Three sittings:
2.00–3.30pm; 3.45–5.15pm; 5.30pm
Set afternoon teas only Traditional Tea, Traditional Tea with Champagne, Seasonal Afternoon Tea
No smoking
Disabled access One small step into the main entrance
Nearest underground stations Piccadilly, Green Park
Parking Public car park nearby
Places of interest nearby Royal Academy of Arts, Green Park, designer shopping on Bond Street

The Drawing Room at Brown's Hotel is a very elegant place to enjoy a special traditional afternoon tea. Resplendent with wood panelling, open fires and graceful antique furnishings, the ambience is reminiscent of an English country house yet the hotel is situated in the very heart of London's Mayfair. Beautiful china, silver tea-ware and linen adorn the tables and tea is served to the accompaniment of soothing piano music. Your personal tiered cake-stand has finger sandwiches, warm scones with clotted cream and strawberry preserve on it, as well as a selection of dainty pastries and home-made cakes, including their famed old-fashioned Victoria sponge cake; you will not want any dinner later. Only leaf tea is served here and besides the familiar varieties there is Brown's special blend – you can buy a caddy of this to take home – and lots of fruit infusions. A very popular place with tourists and locals alike, so don't forget to book your weekday table.

CLARIDGE'S
The Foyer and Reading Room
Brook Street, London W1A 2JQ
Tel 020 7629 8860 ext. 6626
(for tea reservations; recommended to book a week in advance)
Fax 020 7499 2210
e-mail info@claridges.co.uk
www.claridges.co.uk or
www.savoy-group.co.uk

Afternoon tea 3.00–5.30pm
Set afternoon teas only Lady Claridge's Tea, Claridge's Champagne Tea
Smoking permitted, but with discretion
Nearest underground station Bond Street
Parking Meter parking and pay and display nearby
Places of interest nearby Wallace Collection, Bond Street and Regent Street for designer shopping

Art deco fans will be in seventh heaven in Claridge's, for it is, without a doubt, a jewel of a hotel, and owes much of its splendour to the designer Basil Ionides, a 1920s pioneer of the movement. The

Reading Room, with its upholstered chairs and sofas, suede walls and cut marble fireplaces is an alluring place for a very sophisticated afternoon celebration tea. Its companion room, the busier Foyer, is a remarkable blend of marble and mirrors. It features a unique silver-white light sculpture from Seattle-based artist Dale Chihuly. Comprising over 800 individually hand-blown and sculptured pieces it is hung high above a central circular leather banquette and is a definite talking point.

Claridge's are justly proud of their afternoon tea. What an experience it is to be served by liveried footmen. The food, all freshly made under the direction of the *maître chef des cuisines*, is fit for royalty and is unusual without being pretentious. The "Lady Claridge's Tea" is designed to soothe and revive the heartiest shopper or guest; a selection of sandwiches is complemented by the most delicious and unusual apple and raisin scones, served with clotted cream and strawberry preserve, of course. You'll struggle to find room for the exquisite teacakes and pastries which follow and you will probably find it equally difficult to decide which tea to drink, for Claridge's excels by serving 14 different varieties. These all come from the specialist tea supplier, Mariages Frères, who have their own tea salon and tea museum in Paris. Amongst the selection is the unusual "Eros", perfumed with hibiscus and mallow flowers, "Montagne d'Or", perfumed with fruits of China and "Casablanca", an exquisite blend of Moroccan green tea perfumed with mint and bergamot.

Children are welcome at afternoon tea and high chairs are available (advance notice is appreciated). Mobile phones are allowed, but guests are asked to keep the volume down so as not to disturb others.

Visit Claridge's on a weekend afternoon and the duet which plays relaxing music mid-week is replaced by an equally soothing string quartet. All you need to complete the occasion is a glass of exquisite white or pink champagne and then sit back, relax and revel in the ultimate tea experience.

THE CONNAUGHT
The Red Room and Drawing Room
Carlos Place, London W1K AL
Tel 020 7499 7070 (ask for The Red Room or Drawing Room)
Fax 020 7495 3262
e-mail info@the-connaught.co.uk
www.savoy-group.co.uk

Afternoon tea 3.30–5.30pm
Two set afternoon teas Traditional Tea, Celebration Tea; some other options although no full à la carte tea
Smoking permitted, but with discretion (smokers seated away from non-smokers)
Disabled access Limited, there are stairs
Nearest underground stations Bond Street, Green Park, Oxford Circus
Parking Limited meter and pay and display nearby
Places of interest nearby Designer shops on Bond Street, Wallace Collection

The Red Room and Drawing Room, where guests take tea at the imposing Connaught, are everything you would expect from an award-winning hotel in the grand style. The hotel retains its superb Edwardian elegance and is tastefully and comfortably decorated in the best understated English fashion by the designer, Nina Campbell. The Red Room is rather like the lounge of a country house and is somewhat cosier and more intimate than the spacious Drawing Room.

But wherever you sit for tea you can be sure of impeccable, discreet service from staff who really care about your comfort. Fellow guests are as likely to be families as groups of women or business people and many famous names, including Sir Dirk Bogarde, Sir Alec Guinness and Princess

Grace of Monaco have enjoyed the peaceful ambience of tea at The Connaught.

And what a treat the afternoon tea is. The freshest of finger sandwiches are followed by the most delicious warm scones – crisp on the outside, crumbly inside – served with chilled clotted cream and the preserve of your choice. Just to make sure that your scones are warm when they reach your table, they are served covered with a small silver dome. When you are ready – and you won't be rushed – there is a delectable selection of pastries. The tea is poured from silver teapots into the most delightful Limoges china and fresh tea and teacups appear at just the right moment, as if by magic. Quite simply a lovely place to enjoy a traditional afternoon tea.

THE DORCHESTER

The Promenade
Park Lane, London W1A 2HI
Tel 020 7317 6499 (for tea reservations;
bookings recommended for 2.30–3.00pm
only)
Fax 020 7313 6464
e-mail
foodandbeverage@dorchesterhotel.com
www.dorchesterhotel.com

Afternoon tea 2.30–6.00pm
Three set afternoon teas Traditional
Afternoon Tea, Champagne Afternoon Tea,
High Tea; tea à la carte also available
Smoking permitted
Nearest underground station Hyde Park
Corner
Parking None, except by prior arrangement
with the hotel; public car park nearby
Places of interest nearby Apsley House,
Buckingham Palace, Albert Memorial,
Victoria and Albert Museum, Museum of
Mankind, shopping in Knightsbridge and
Bond Street

Taking afternoon tea in The Promenade,
the focal point of The Dorchester since it
opened in 1931, has to be one of the most
pleasurable and special tea experiences
imaginable. Besides indulging oneself in
the most sumptuous tea, the décor is
stunningly opulent, the ambience serene
and the service impeccable.

Your afternoon of sheer luxury begins as
soon as you sink into one of the lounge's
cosy sofas, or settle on a silk damask
upholstered chair. Here you are surrounded
by acres of marble, gilded columns,
luxurious carpets, Regency mirrors and
marble-topped tables. Great attention has
been paid to every detail, from the elegant
linen and silverware to the fine china, so
that you feel really pampered.

The Dorchester's award-winning
afternoon tea combines tradition with
excellence. A daily-changing selection of six
sorts of finger sandwiches, freshly-baked
warm scones and delectable French pastries
from the *patissier's* presentation platter are
served on a silver, tiered stand. Add a glass
of champagne to this and you have a truly
celebratory tea. Whilst the most popular tea
is "The Dorchester House Blend" a selection
of more than 30 leaf teas is available and as
you would expect from a venue of this
calibre, many of these are rare varieties.

Tea in The Promenade at The Dorchester
is a truly memorable occasion. The hotel
will even arrange birthday cakes and flowers
if you are celebrating a special occasion. It is
hardly surprising that guests are as reluctant
to leave as they are eager to arrive.

FORTNUM & MASON

St James's Restaurant
181 Piccadilly, London W1A 1ER
Tel 020 7734 8040
Fax 020 7437 3278
e-mail info@fortnumandmason.co.uk
www.fortnumandmason.co.uk

Afternoon tea 3.00–5.15pm (store opening hours differ); closed on Sunday and Bank holidays
Three set teas High Tea, Traditional Afternoon Tea, Cream Tea
Smoking permitted
Nearest underground stations Green Park, Piccadilly
Places of interest nearby Buckingham Palace, Royal Academy of Arts, Bond Street, Burlington Arcade

Crossing the threshold into Fortnum & Mason – famed for its chiming clock – is like stepping into an Aladdin's cave, for the ground floor is filled with the most sublime displays of extraordinarily luxurious food. This should give you an inkling of the treat that awaits you at teatime.

A number of restaurants within the store serve afternoon tea, but the most elegant is, without doubt, the St James's Restaurant on the fourth floor. The tables are laid with linen and fine china and three set tea menus are on offer. For the greediest (or hungriest) guest there is the High Tea – a positive feast of Fortnum's famous Welsh Rarebit or Scrambling Highlander (scrambled eggs and smoked salmon on granary bread) followed by scones, Somerset clotted cream and strawberry preserve, followed by afternoon cakes from the in-house patisserie. A choice of delicious sandwiches appears on the Traditional Afternoon Tea menu alongside the scones, cakes and tea, whilst the Cream Tea is relatively restrained, just scones, cream and jam, a slice of home-made almond cake and tea. Add a glass of champagne to any of these for a really special occasion. The choice of teas on offer has to be the crowning glory to this marathon of food, for Fortnum's has an unsurpassed reputation as a supplier of exceptional quality teas. The rare tea selection includes Assam Mangalam, Darjeeling Chamong and the extremely rare Fines Keemun Hao Ya, whilst the leaf tea selection list features, amongst others, Royal Blend, Queen Anne Blend and Darjeeling Broken Orange Pekoe.

On your way out be sure to browse around the astonishing foodhall and perhaps purchase one of the hundred or so teas on sale there.

FOUR SEASONS HOTEL

The Lounge
Hamilton Place, London W1A 1AZ
Tel 020 7499 0888 ext. 5334 (for tea
reservations)
Fax 020 7493 1895
e-mail fsh.london@fourseasons.com
www.fourseasons.com

Afternoon tea 3.00–7.00pm
Three set afternoon teas Devonshire Tea,
Seasonal Afternoon Tea, Celebration Tea;
tea à la carte also available
Smoking permitted
Nearest underground stations Hyde Park,
Piccadilly
Parking Hotel car park (payable)
Places of interest nearby Hyde Park,
Knightsbridge, Apsley House

Many guests still refer to the Four Seasons
Hotel by its original name, The Inn on the
Park – a testimony to the loyalty they feel
towards this modern but immensely
traditional hotel. Renowned for the
attention to personal service, the ambience
in The Lounge is one of relaxed comfort,
with sofas and settees set in conversational
groups for intimacy.

Apart from the Devonshire Tea with its
sandwiches, scones and tea, the other
award-winning set teas at the Four Seasons
are far from traditional English fare and are
designed to tantalize the taste buds. Four
adventurous new tea menus are created
every year by the executive chef, each
reflecting a particular season and

incorporating seasonal produce. Spring Tea
might include mango scones and rhubarb
jam and sandwich fillings as diverse as
marinated salmon with lime or courgette
and mint brouillade, served in home-baked
bread, made with mustard, lime, tomato or
fig. Special occasions receive regular
attention and are marked with a
celebration tea such as "Queen Mother's
Afternoon Tea" in honour of her 100th
birthday. There is a splendid range of leaf
teas on offer, including China Black,
Green Gunpowder, Queen Mary (a
Darjeeling blend that was the personal
choice of the late Queen Mary) and
Twinings specially created (Silver)
Anniversary Blend. Taking tea at this hotel
is a real treat for a special celebration.

HARRODS

The Georgian Restaurant
Brompton Road, London SW1X 7XL
Tel 020 7225 6800 (for tea bookings)
Fax 020 7225 5903
e-mail catering@harrods.com
www.Harrods.com

Afternoon Tea 3.30–7.00pm Monday–
Saturday (store opening hours differ)
Two set teas Best Afternoon Tea in
London, Champagne Afternoon Tea
Smoking at designated tables only
Nearest underground station
Knightsbridge
Parking Store car park (payable)
Places of interest nearby Sloane Street for
designer boutiques, Victoria and Albert
Museum, Natural History Museum, Science
Museum, Royal Albert Hall, Hyde Park

Of the 20 restaurants within Harrods,
Britains largest department store, the
Georgian Restaurant is undoubtedly the
flagship. The décor is every bit as grand as
when Victor Silvester, the great band
leader, had tea here in the 1930s and the
resident pianist, who plays every day, adds
to your enjoyment.

Full afternoon tea arrives very grandly on
a silver stand and is a lovely selection of
mini sandwiches, Harrods scones with
clotted cream and preserves and dainty tea
pastries. The menu choice of Harrods tea
includes their own Afternoon Blend and
the ever popular Darjeeling, Lapsang
Souchong and Assam, but you are invited
to ask for any other unlisted variety that
you especially like. For tea connoisseurs
this could be heaven, as the store, which
originally opened as a tea merchant and
grocery store in 1849, sells an enviable
range of thirst-quenching premium blends
in the magnificent Food Hall, over 160
varieties. One exclusive is Hand-Twisted
Organic Darjeeling, but as this is only
available in very limited quantities, it is
unlikely to ever feature on the afternoon
tea menu. Console yourself instead with a
purchase from the caddy collection –
second flush Darjeeling Margaret's Hope or
Castleton perhaps.

Harrods operate a strict dress code – no
ripped jeans or scruffy clothing and mobile
phones are banned throughout the store.
Harrods is a hive of activity, and The
Georgian Restaurant may not be as quiet as
some visitors would like. However, you can
be sure of the most courteous and warm
attention from the waiting staff, whose aim
is to make your visit a memorable and
enjoyable occasion, even offering the
accompanying baby ice cream!

HARVEY NICHOLS
The Fifth Floor Café
109-125 Knightsbridge, London SW1X 7RJ
Tel 020 7823 1839 (Café direct line for bookings)
Fax 020 823 2207
www.harveynichols.com

Afternoon tea 3.30–6.00pm Monday–Saturday (store opening hours differ)
Set afternoon tea or tea à la carte available
Smoking permitted in designated areas
Nearest underground station Knightsbridge
Parking Limited pay and display in area
Places of interest nearby Sloane Street for designer shopping, Hyde Park

The Fifth Floor Café at "Harvey Nicks" is just the place for fashion aficionados and celebrity spotters to take afternoon tea – Geri Halliwell and Gwyneth Paltrow, amongst many others, have been seen here. Everything about the modern and dramatic interior – metal, glass, vibrant colours, space and lots of natural light – reflects the up-to-the-minute style of this designer-led store. The atmosphere is noisy and lively – including the regular ringing of mobile phones – so it's probably not the place to take an elderly granny for her birthday tea, but tradition still rules as far as the set afternoon tea is concerned. This includes a scone, clotted cream and jam as well as a choice of cake or tart. There is a select range of bagged teas on offer – English

Breakfast, Earl Grey, Assam, Darjeeling and Lapsang, as well as some herbal and fruit varieties. Whether you go for the lemon tart, chocolate éclair or other delicious confection, forget counting the calories and instead contemplate which variety of tea or other desirable comestible you can buy in the very chic foodmarket, adjacent. The ultimate place to have a "designer" tea.

KENSINGTON PALACE
The Orangery
Kensington Gardens, London W8 4PX
Tel 020 7376 0239
Fax 020 7376 0198
www.hrp.org.uk

Afternoon tea 3.00–5pm November–March; 3.00–6.00pm April–October
Three set afternoon teas Victorian Tea, Orangery Tea, Grand Tea; tea à la carte also available
No smoking

Nearest underground stations Queensway, Gloucester Road, High Street Kensington
Parking Public car park on Bayswater Road
Places of interest nearby Kensington Palace, Serpentine Gallery, Princess Diana Memorial Playground, Kensington Gardens

The magnificent eighteenth-century Orangery, situated within the grounds of Kensington Palace where Queen Victoria was born, is a busy and bustling place for tea, but one which retains its sense of history and grandeur. Sitting here, amidst the tranquil haven of Kensington Gardens, you can almost imagine Queen Anne and her aristocratic guests dining here in the summer months.

A heavily laden table of delectable home-made scones, shortbreads, fruit slices and wholesome cakes greets you as you walk in the door and you'll find it quite a challenge deciding what to eat. You could always settle for one of the set teas rather than ordering à la carte; perhaps the Grand Tea, which includes a glass of champagne. Two varieties of bagged tea, four of leaf and four fruit infusions are on offer. Masons Old Chelsea china and flowers on the tables, which are well spaced, add to the ambience and the waiting staff are friendly and helpful. It is very popular with families, probably because of the Princess Diana Memorial Playground located nearby.

The slight drawbacks of the Orangery is that at busy times you may have to queue outside and the toilets are situated in a separate small building a short walk away. These things aside, you can expect to pass a very pleasant couple of hours and you could, of course, visit the palace afterwards.

KENWOOD HOUSE

The Brew House Restaurant
Hampstead Lane, London NW3 3JR
Tel 020 8348 2528
Fax 020 8348 2643
e-mail enquiries@kenwoodhospitality.co.uk

Afternoon tea 9.00am–4.00pm October–March; 9.00am–6.00pm April–September
Tea à la carte only
No smoking
Nearest underground stations Hampstead Heath, Highgate
Parking At Kenwood House
Places of interest nearby Hampstead Heath, Keats House

I'm an enthusiastic walker and the Brew House, set in the service wing of Kenwood House, is a wonderful place for a rest and refreshment after a long trek across Hampstead Heath. It is also very popular with locals and visitors to the house itself, an imposing eighteenth-century villa which houses the Iveagh Bequest, an internationally renowned collection of paintings you should try to visit if you have time. Take a look at the walls in the Brew House while you are deciding what to eat, for they have been cleverly decorated to resemble a Print Room, but all the vistas and views are *trompe l'oeil* – a "trick of the eye".

This self-service restaurant offers deliciously wholesome, home-made food, but there is no set tea menu. At any time of the day you can expect to find baskets piled high with jumbo scones, served with whipped cream and preserves and cakes such as chocolate fudge, carrot and sticky toffee date. Cream cakes and Danish pastries add to the temptation, so resist if you can! Bagged tea comes from a long-established supplier in nearby Muswell Hill and besides the old favourites – Assam and Earl Grey – you can select Gunpowder green tea and organic Ceylon.

On a dry, bright day the outside terrace with its landscaped garden is a delightful place to sit, gossip and sip your tea. Just be sure to wrap up warm in the winter!

THE KEW GREENHOUSE

1 Station Parade, Kew Gardens, Surrey
TW9 3PS
Tel 020 8940 0183

Opening hours 9.00am–dusk
Tea à la carte
Smoking permitted except for in conservatory gallery
Nearest underground station Kew Gardens
Parking On-street parking
Places of interest nearby Royal Botanic Gardens

The Kew Greenhouse, resplendent with its abundance of foliage and greenery, was built in 1895 and served as the village bakery for many years before eventually evolving into a fully-fledged tearoom and café-restaurant. Many original fittings, including the vast brick ovens with their ornate cast iron doors and royal coat of arms, have been lovingly preserved, and these add to the ambience of the place. The atmosphere is far from formal and you get what the owners describe as "proper food and cake", all home-baked. You have to order at the counter but your food – perhaps including their award-winning scones – is then brought to the table. Both leaf and bagged tea are served; the range includes the usual favourites as well as some 20 or more herbal teas and infusions. In the summer, striped awnings and umbrellas on the piazza shade you from the sun. Not the place for a celebration tea, but somewhere you can be sure you will get fresh, wholesome food and a refreshing pot of tea.

THE LANDMARK LONDON
Winter Garden
222 Marylebone Road, London NW1 6JQ
Tel 020 7631 8000 (no bookings taken)
Fax 020 7631 8080
e-mail reservations@thelandmark.co.uk
www.landmarklondon.co.uk

Afternoon tea 3.00–6.00pm
Two set afternoon teas or tea à la carte (hotel operates a minimum charge for non-residents, check when ordering)
Designated smoking areas
Nearest underground station Marylebone
Parking Underground parking for 80 cars, meters and pay and display nearby
Places of interest nearby Madame Tussauds, The Planetarium

Walking into the Winter Garden at the Landmark London, with its soaring glass-roofed eight-storey atrium, palm trees and amazing feeling of light and space, is a breathtaking experience. Originally opened in 1899 as one of the great Victorian railway termini hotels – the Winter Garden was the vast central courtyard – it still retains the character, elegance and grandeur of a bygone era. Despite its popularity and informality, there is an aura of comfortable, calm perfection about the place (mobile phones are discouraged), an ambience which is reflected in the beautifully served, award-winning afternoon tea.

The tea here is a positive feast and everything is freshly prepared on the day, in the hotel's own pastry department.

Assorted sandwiches and dainty Viennese bridge rolls, plain and fruit scones with clotted cream and strawberry jam, compete with delicious home-baked tea-breads, crumpets, toasted currant teacakes and elegant French pastries for room on your plate. The Landmark Tea, one of the two set teas on offer, includes strawberries and cream and champagne and is tailor-made for that extra special occasion. With a choice of over 30 leaf teas, including Lapsang Souchong, Green Gunpowder, Russian Caravan, Darjeeling, Assam and Earl Grey Blue Flower as well as tisanes, exotic black teas and fruit infusions, there is a tea to suit every taste. The gentle and relaxing strains of a grand piano, accompanied by a violin or flute, add to the pleasure of tea in the Winter Garden, which is a truly delightful experience.

THE LANESBOROUGH
The Conservatory
1 Lanesborough Place, Hyde Park Corner,
London SW1X 7TA
Tel 020 7259 5599 (ask for the Conservatory)
Fax 020 7259 5606
e-mail info@lanesborough.co.uk
www.lanesborough.co.uk

Afternoon tea 3.30–6.00pm Monday–Saturday; 4.00–6.00pm Sunday
Two set teas or tea à la carte (minimum charge applies)
Smoking permitted (room is air-conditioned)
Nearest underground station Hyde Park Corner
Parking Hotel valet parking
Places of interest nearby Hyde Park, Knightsbridge, Admiralty Arch, Apsley House

As you walk into the Lanesborough's glass-roofed Conservatory the striking décor of soaring palms, Chinese lanterns and Oriental figurines momentarily transports you to the exotic and mystical East. Gentle piano music accompanies your afternoon tea, which is as unique an experience as the surroundings. Whether you choose the Lanesborough Tea – delicious home-made traditional fare plus crumpets and English tea-breads, the Belgravia Tea – the Lanesborough with the addition of strawberries, cream and a glass of champagne, an afternoon champagne cocktail or tea à la carte, you'll be served with courtesy. Drinking tea here is well worthwhile, for the Lanesborough prides itself on a daily tasting of their teas to ensure quality and consistency of flavour. The list includes some unusual varieties of leaf such as Rose Congou and Lychee as well as their unique and exclusive Afternoon Blend. Only leaf tea is served here, but there is not a tea strainer in sight. The secret lies in the strainer ingeniously fitted inside the teapot.

So, whether you are exhausted from a day's shopping in nearby Knightsbridge or just want to relax, unwind or treat yourself to a glorious afternoon tea in an unusual but very comfortable setting, the Conservatory is to be recommended.

LOUIS PATISSERIE
32 Heath Street, Hampstead, London
NW3 6TE
Tel 020 7435 9908

Opening hours 9.00am–6.00pm
Tea à la carte
Smoking permitted
Nearest underground station Hampstead
Parking Pay and display nearby
Places of interest nearby Historic Hampstead Village, Hampstead Heath, Keats' House, Fenton House

Louis Patisserie is a real institution in Hampstead and the shop's distinctive pink cartons and bags can be seen all around the area. The tiny tea lounge, which was founded in 1963 by Louis Permayer, retains a charming old-fashioned, continental feel and is regularly patronized by the local literati, thespians and singers. Louis's personal influence is very evident for he continues to work in the bakery attached to the tea lounge. You can eat here at any time of the day, but for your teatime treat choose from the extensive daily selection of croissants, Danish pastries, fruit tarts, meringues, scones and cream cakes. All of these and more, are temptingly displayed in the window and everything is freshly baked on the premises. Four different types of tea, both leaf and bagged, are available and are served in china cups and saucers. An informal place to relax and rest when shopping or sightseeing. You can always buy a little something to take home with you as well.

THE MONTAGUE ON THE GARDENS

The Conservatory
15 Montague Square, Bloomsbury, London
WC1B 5BJ
Tel 020 7612 8414 (for tea reservations)
Fax 020 7637 2516
e-mail reservations@montague.
redcarnation hotels.com
www.redcarnationhotels.com

Afternoon tea 3.00–6.00pm
Two set teas Cream Tea, High Tea; tea à la
carte also available
No smoking
Nearest underground stations Russell
Square, Holborn
Parking Limited meter parking in area
Places of interest nearby British Museum,
Covent Garden

The time-honoured tradition of afternoon
tea is celebrated every afternoon in the
delightful sunlit conservatory of the
Montague on the Gardens. Overlooking a
peaceful and secluded garden square and
adjacent to the world famous British
Museum, the conservatory is also ideally
situated for visitors to literary Bloomsbury
and Covent Garden. Comfort and luxury
are combined in these charming
surroundings, and the tea is a positive
pleasure. Silverware, china and flowers
adorn the tables and only the finest leaf tea
is served, although the range of 10 teas
available is fairly standard. As well as tea à
la carte there are two set teas to choose
between – a traditional Cream Tea of

freshly-baked scones, jam and that most
slimming of toppings, Devonshire clotted
cream, or High Tea, which, in addition, has
finger sandwiches and pastries of the day.
Very comforting food indeed. In the
summer the garden terrace is a delightful
place to take tea.

NATIONAL PORTRAIT GALLERY

The Portrait Restaurant
Orange Street, London WC2 0HE
Tel 020 7636 1555 (bookings for large
parties on 020 7312 2490)
Fax 020 7925 0244
e-mail portrait.restaurant@talk21.com
www.searcys.co.uk

Afternoon tea 3.00–5.00pm
Two set teas Light Tea, High Tea; tea à la
carte also available
No smoking
Nearest underground stations Leicester
Square, Charing Cross
No parking

Places of interest nearby Covent Garden, National Gallery, Trafalgar Square, Piccadilly Circus

The vista from this restaurant, where a very good traditional afternoon tea is served every day, is not so much a "portrait" as a "landscape", and a spectacular one at that. No matter where you sit in this stylish modern room, you get a panoramic view of Nelson's Column, Big Ben and the Houses of Parliament, which makes it one of London's hidden treasures.

If you want scones here, you'll have to go for one of the set teas – one misleadingly called Light Tea, which is a calorie-laden plate of two large, fluffy scones accompanied by a scoop of golden clotted cream and jam. A boozier version of this, no less fattening, includes a glass of champagne. Only bagged tea is served here and you'll have to ask for hot water. The staff are young, the service artistically indifferent and if you sit near the bar and service area, it can be a bit noisy. Still, the atmosphere is very relaxed, the tea is good and it's a super place to rest after a visit to the stunning Portrait Gallery rooms downstairs. Even on a dull wet day a visit here is an energizing experience.

THE ORIGINAL MAIDS OF HONOUR
288 Kew Road, Richmond, Surrey
TW9 3DU
Tel 020 8940 2752

Afternoon tea 2.30–5.30pm Tuesday–Saturday
One set tea or tea à la carte
No smoking
Nearest underground station Kew Gardens
Parking On-street parking
Places of interest nearby Royal Botanic Gardens, Public Record Office

For many visitors, The Original Maids of Honour is exactly what a teashop should be – quaint, quirky and quintessentially English. The old world, nostalgic feel is everywhere, from the bow-fronted windows, chintz curtains, open log fire, oak tables and wheelback chairs to the crocheted lace doilies, willow pattern china and collection of teapots. There's a small terrace with tables outside where you can sip your tea on a nice summer day.

The Maids of Honour cake, after which the shop is named, is a real curiosity and worth a try. Legend has it that King Henry VIII ate these cakes whilst he was at Richmond Palace and liked them so much that he ordered that the recipe be locked in

an iron box and kept secret. It remains a Newens' family secret to this day. You know that the fluffy scones are home-made – like everything else here – because they are delightfully different shapes. On busy days you may be asked to share a table and you can then compare notes about the lovely cakes and pastries.

PATISSERIE VALERIE AT SAGNE

105 Marylebone High Street, London W1M 3DB
Tel 020 7935 3698/6240/6974
Fax 020 7935 6543
e-mail info@patisserie-valerie.co.uk
www.patisserie-valerie.co.uk

Opening hours 7.30am–7.00pm Monday–Friday; 8.00am–7.00pm Saturday; 9.00am–6.00pm Sunday and Bank Holidays
One set tea Madame Valerie's Cream Tea; tea à la carte

Smoking permitted in designated areas
Nearest underground stations Baker Street, Bond Street
Parking Meter or pay and display in High Street and adjacent roads
Places of interest nearby Madame Tussauds, London Planetarium, Oxford Street

You could very easily imagine that you are *en France* in Patisserie Valerie, for the character and food are very continental. The wonderful window display will certainly tempt you inside to a café resplendent with 1920s Palladian murals and gold-leaf chandeliers. With seating for 80 at comfortable wooden tables and chairs, the ambience is busy, lively and very relaxed and it is easy to see why the place is so popular with local residents, tourists and business people alike. I'm told it is also a favourite haunt of theatrical people – but discretion prevents anyone being named.

Valerie's, which was originally founded in 1926, is a famous rendezvous for most excellent French pastries: chocolate or coffee éclairs, doughnuts filled with jam or *crème* patisserie, individual lemon, apple, pear, strawberry or raspberry tarts, assorted *millefeuille* – the list is endless and all are quite irresistible. If you are a traditionalist, Madame Valerie can provide you with excellent toasted (or not, if you prefer) scones, clotted cream and preserves. Loose leaf tea is the order of the day and 14 varieties in all are served, including Russian Caravan and China Apple; and you'll get a pot of hot water served with your tea. Splendid celebration cakes are made to

order on the premises, as are the hand-made chocolates – a tempting addition to a good, "meet your friends for a chat" kind of tea.

PETER DE WIT'S CAFÉ

21 Greenwich Church Street, London SE10 9BJ
Tel/Fax 020 8305 0048
e-mail toymaker@btinternet.com

Opening hours 12.00 noon–6.00pm Tuesday–Friday; 10.00am–7.00pm Saturday, Sunday and Bank holidays
Cream tea and tea à la carte
Smoking tolerated, but with courtesy
Nearest underground station North Greenwich

Parking Public car parks nearby
Places of interest nearby Cutty Sark, National Maritime Museum, Greenwich Old Royal Observatory, Fan Museum, Rangers House

A treasure in the midst of historic Greenwich and very popular with tourists, is the de Wit's tiny café situated within the oldest house in the district. Dating back, in part, to the fifteenth century, the interior is plain and simple but you can be sure of a warm welcome and excellent service from the young, enthusiastic staff. The emphasis is on quality and only the finest, often organic, ingredients are used in the preparation of their food. Scones are served with unsalted French butter, double or clotted cream and preserves, the huge sandwiches have classic fillings and the home-baked cakes are served in pudding size portions. Expect to find Carrot Cake and Apple Crumble Cake, both favourites, as well as a light and a rich fruit cake.

There are five Indian and two China teas to choose from as well as a range of herbal and fruit infusions. Even though tables are in demand at the weekends, you won't find yours being cleared as soon as you finish the last crumb of cake. Weekdays are certainly more leisurely and you can linger as long as you like, do the crossword or play chess whilst you enjoy the interesting background music. There are so many tourist attractions in the vicinity that you could have a light lunch here and then return for a scrumptious tea later in the day.

THE RITZ

The Palm Court

150 Piccadilly, London W1J 9BR

Tel 020 7493 8181 (reservations essential, at least four weeks in advance)

Fax 020 7493 2687

e-mail enquire@theritzlondon

www.theritzlondon.com (for on-line tea bookings)

Afternoon tea 12.00 noon–2.00pm "first come, first served"; three sittings: 2.00pm, 3.30pm and 5.00pm

One set tea

No smoking

Disabled access A few steps up to the Palm Court

Nearest underground stations Green Park, Piccadilly

Parking Valet parking

Places of interest nearby Royal Academy of Arts, Green Park, Saville Row, Burlington Arcade, Bond Street

The world famous Palm Court in Cesar Ritz's gracious Edwardian hotel, located in the heart of St James's, is the epitome of sophistication and elegance and the afternoon tea the height of decadence and luxury. You know that you are about to enjoy a very special experience as you take the few steps up to the Palm Court from the ground floor's central gallery area, passing between a pair of grand Ionic marbled columns. Pretty Louis XVI chairs, marble-topped tables beautifully set with crisp linen and delicate china await the

guests eager to share in what is a quintessentially Ritz experience.

If you are an aspiring tea guest, you must book your table several weeks in advance. I can promise you that the wait will be well worth it, for the afternoon tea is quite superb, the service very attentive and although you will be limited to how long you can stay by the next sitting, there is no real sense of pressure on you to "eat up". Alongside the selection of dainty sandwiches made on different breads are freshly-baked scones, clotted cream and home-made strawberry jam, tea pastries and fresh cream cakes. It's impossible to leave feeling hungry, as the Ritz feast is regularly replenished by the staff. A choice from seven varieties of leaf tea completes the occasion, for an "occasion" is exactly what tea in the Palm Court is. When you

start to suffer from "Ritz" withdrawal symptoms, you'll find the recipe for their wonderful Marble Cake and other delectable items in *The London Ritz Book of Afternoon Tea.*

There is a strict dress code; jeans are not allowed and gentlemen must wear a jacket and tie. Mobile phones are discouraged.

THE RUBENS AT THE PALACE
The Palace Lounge
39 Buckingham Palace Road, London SW1W 0PS
Tel 020 7834 6600 (booking recommended)
Fax 020 7828 5401
e-mail sales@rubens.redcarnationhotels.com
www.redcarnationhotel.com

Afternoon tea 2.30–5.00pm
Traditional set afternoon tea or tea à la carte
No smoking
Nearest underground station Victoria
Parking Public car park near Victoria coach station, meters and pay and display in Warwick Row and Bressenden Place
Places of interest nearby Buckingham Palace, Green Park, St James's Park

Just a stone's throw from Buckingham Palace, close by beautiful St James's Park, Green Park, The Mall and with a view of Buckingham Palace Royal Mews, the Palace Lounge at The Rubens is a very enticing

haven for a highly-rated traditional afternoon tea. Comfortable wing chairs and sofas add to the relaxed but refined atmosphere and the service is efficient and attentive but discreet. This probably explains why the lounge was so popular in the 1940s with General Sikorski, Commander-in-Chief of the Free Polish Forces, who took tea here every day, accompanied on one occasion by General de Gaulle.

Afternoon tea consists of finger sandwiches, scones and Devonshire clotted cream – or toasted teacake if you prefer – with preserves. These and the tea pastries, which are all home-made, are presented on an elegant tiered silver stand. Your tea – you can request either leaf or bagged and choose from 10 different varieties – is served in a silver teapot and accompanied by the all important jug of hot water. If you are visiting in the summer, why not visit Buckingham Palace first, then after your delicious tea take a stroll to Westminster, Harrods or the London Eye.

SAVOY

THE SAVOY
Thames Foyer
Strand, London WC2R 0EU
Tel 020 7836 4343 (booking advisable for
afternoon tea and tea dances)
Fax 020 7240 6040
e-mail info@the-savoy.co.uk
www.savoy-group.co.uk

Afternoon tea 3.00–5.30pm Monday–
Saturday; Tea dance 3.00–5.30pm Sunday
One set tea
**Smoking allowed, but a "with courtesy"
policy is applied**
Disabled access Limited, stairs down to
Foyer
Nearest underground stations Charing
Cross, Covent Garden, Embankment
Parking Adelphi Garage nearby
Places of interest nearby Somerset
House, Festival Hall, National Theatre,
Savoy Theatre, Covent Garden, Royal
Opera House

As you descend the elegant staircase to the
Thames Foyer of the Savoy you can't help
but notice an aura of restrained elegance
and grandeur, evocative of times past. The
décor is wonderful, from the *trompe l'oeil*
mural of a romantic garden to the three
spectacular art deco mirrors which adorn
another wall. It was in these marvellous
surroundings that Rudolph Valentino
danced and where George Gershwin
played *Rhapsody In Blue*. The tranquil
ambience is complemented by the discreet
but totally attentive service and guests may
linger in the deep sofas and armchairs for
as long as they like, whilst listening to the
delicate strains of the piano. The set tea of
delicate finger sandwiches, delectable bite-
size French pastries, plain and fruit scones

– all made in the hotel's patisserie – served with clotted cream and strawberry preserve, arrives on a three-tiered silver stand, served by waiters in tail coats. Don't worry if you can't finish all the cakes – a "doggy" bag can easily be arranged! Guests are requested not to wear denim or trainers.

Connoisseurs of tea will be spoilt for choice as the Savoy offers a distinctive collection of leaf teas. Besides their own blend, special teas and speciality blends from Newby and Mariages Frères include Marco Polo, Casablanca, Assam second flush and the highly prized Darjeeling first and second flush. On Sunday afternoons the *faux* wall with the mural is folded back to reveal a dance floor and guests can recapture the 1920s pleasure of the *thé dansant*, which owes so much of its history to The Savoy. Taking tea here is a quintessentially English experience and one not to be missed. If you feel in need of a souvenir, why not buy a copy of Anton Edelman's book, *Taking Tea at the Savoy*, before you leave?

ST MARTIN'S LANE HOTEL

Tuscan
St Martin's Lane, London WC2N 4HX
Tel 020 7311 1444 (for restaurant and bookings)
www.tuscan-restaurant.com

Afternoon tea 3.00–5.00pm
One set tea
Smoking allowed

Nearest underground stations Leicester Square, Covent Garden, Piccadilly Circus
Parking Public car park nearby
Places of interest nearby Theatreland, Trafalgar Square, National Gallery, National Portrait Gallery, Covent Garden

If you are looking for a stylish, up-to-the-minute venue for tea rather than old-world grandeur, then look no further than Tuscan at the St Martin's Lane Hotel or Spoon at its sister hotel, Sanderson. Modern, minimalist décor, created by the world renowned designer, Philippe Starck, sets the scene for a traditional English tea, complete with tiered stand, but with a refreshing and innovative continental twist. The young and enthusiastic staff serve you with freshly-prepared, delectable Italian-style sandwiches – speciality bread with fillings such as roasted peppers, pesto and mozzarella – followed by the most excellent scones, jam and clotted cream. Should you have any room left after this, then you'll be offered a selection of delicious cakes and individual pastries which might include chocolate biscuit cake, melt-in-the-mouth lemon curd tart, mini pavlova or a slice of ginger cake. A good selection of teas, leaf and bagged, are on offer, and why not add some sparkle to tea with a glass of strawberry Bellini or pink champagne? Taking tea at Tuscan is very twenty-first century, but it's a great place to enjoy an award-winning tea in comfortable modern surroundings and who knows which famous person you might bump into.

Rest of Britain

AVON

PUMP ROOM RESTAURANT

9 Stall Street, Bath BA1 1LZ
Tel 01225 444477
Fax 01225 447979
e-mail pumproom@milburn.co.uk
www.milburn.co.uk

Opening hours 9.30am; closing times vary
according to the time of year, check with
Pump Room
Six set afternoon teas Champagne Tea,
Bath Tea, Pump Room Tea, Spa High Tea,
Beau Nash Cream Tea, Georgian Cream
Tea; tea à la carte also available
Designated smoking areas
Location Opposite Bath Abbey, within the
Roman Baths building
Parking Several public car parks nearby
Places of interest nearby The Abbey,
Roman Baths, Pump Room, Costume
Museum, Royal Crescent

The Pump Room has been Bath's favourite
meeting place since the eighteenth century
when fashionable society congregated here
to socialize and "take the waters". The
elegance and classical Georgian charm of
the room has hardly changed since it was
built and it's no wonder that Jane Austen
sent the heroine of her novel *Persuasion*
here in the hope of bumping into her beau.
Whilst the fictional Catherine and Mr
Tilney may have sampled the spa water –
which visitors may still do – it's doubtful
that they would have enjoyed the varieties
of set teas which are served here now.

Seated at tables set with crisp linen under
a wonderful glass chandelier, you can enjoy
one of six slightly unusual set teas. Finger
sandwiches and scones, Bath buns and
Dundee cakes, and even Welsh rarebit are
served. Pump Room cakes and pastries, all
freshly home-baked, might include
wholesome Polish honey cake, coffee and
pecan layer cake or rich fruit cake in winter
– the selection changes monthly, so you
can make regular visits and never get bored.
Bagged teas on offer are English Breakfast,
Assam, Darjeeling, Lapsang Souchong and
Ceylon, as well as a selection of herbal teas.
Add to all this the tinkling of a piano or
the strains of the Pump Room Trio playing
in the background and your delightful
afternoon tea is complete.

BERKSHIRE

CASTLE HOTEL

Pennington Lounge
High Street, Windsor SL4 ILJ
Tel 0870 400 8300/01753 851011
(booking recommended)
Fax 01753 830244
e-mail castle@heritage-hotels.co.uk
www.heritage-hotels.co.uk

Afternoon tea 3.00–6.00pm (or any other
time on request)
Three set afternoon teas Cream Tea,
Castle Afternoon Tea, Royal Afternoon Tea
(includes champagne)
Smoking permitted
Location In town centre, opposite castle

Parking Private car park accessible from driveway down the side of the hotel
Places of interest nearby Windsor Castle, Eton College, Hampton Court, Runnymede, Windsor Great Park, Legoland, Dorney Court, Virginia Water, Theatre Royal, Savill Gardens, Thorpe Park

The Castle Hotel, set right in the heart of historic Windsor, was built in 1528 as a coaching inn and was originally known as The Mermaid. It's a fine example of Georgian architecture and a refined place to take afternoon tea. The Pennington Lounge is a relaxing and comfortable room and has the additional benefit of giving one of the best vantage points to watch the splendid "Changing of the Guard" parade. You could arrive for morning coffee and view this spectacle, visit Windsor Castle – the oldest royal residence to stay in constant use by monarchs of England – then return later for tea.

Your afternoon tea is served in style – a three-tiered silver cake-stand laden with delicious finger sandwiches, scones and dainty pastries – accompanied by a pot of one of the usual teas. An exceptionally civilized experience.

CAMBRIDGESHIRE
THE LITTLE TEA ROOM
1 All Saints Passage, Cambridge CB2 3LT
Tel 01223 319393
Fax 01223 366722
e-mail glene@onetel.net.uk

Opening hours 10.00am–5.30pm
Traditional cream tea and extensive à la carte menu
No smoking
Disabled access There are three steps into the tearoom
Location All Saints Passage runs from the end of Jesus Lane to Trinity Street and is located opposite St Johns and Trinity Colleges
Parking Public car parks in city centre
Places of interest nearby Historic colleges, Fitzwilliam Museum, the "Backs"

You get an overwhelming sense of history whilst sipping tea in the charming Little Tea Room. The building dates back to the 1500s and is squeezed into All Saints Passage, a stone's throw from Trinity and St John's, two of Cambridge's largest colleges. There is a very picturesque garden next door which often hosts a craft market and if you sit in the front parlour you can watch the world go by. Inside, blue and white chinaware is on display everywhere and is for sale. You can stop for a bite to eat any time of day, but teatime is particularly tempting. Tradition rules with the familiar cream tea and a delicious Victoria sponge. But be bold and try the chocolate fudge or zesty orange drizzle cake – all home-baked. Try and resist the special cakes – warm chocolate fudge brownie with fudge sauce and ice cream or delicious ginger cake with hot maple syrup and cream – mouth-watering! Leaf tea includes Earl Grey, Lady Grey Assam and other popular varieties.

CHESHIRE
KATIE'S TEA ROOMS
38 Watergate Street, Chester CH1 2LA
Tel 01244 400322
Fax 01244 400991

Opening hours 10.00am–10.00pm
Tuesday–Saturday; 10.00am–5.00pm
Sunday–Monday
Set afternoon tea and extensive tea à la carte menu
Designated smoking areas
Disabled access Limited
Location Chester city centre; locate
Chester Cross, follow Watergate Street
leading from the Cross; shop is on right-
hand side
Parking Public car parks nearby
Places of interest nearby Chester Roman
City, Chester Cathedral, Chester Castle,
Toy Museum, Chester Zoo

Silver teapots brimming with one of ten
speciality leaf teas and three-tiered cake-
stands laden with finger sandwiches, fruit
scones and slices of cake, await you in
Katie's Tea Rooms in historic Chester. The
black and white Grade 1 listed building is
over 600 years old and has entrances from
both street level and from the Chester
Rows – through the magnificent original
studded oak door – the galleried tiers of
shops for which the medieval walled city is
so famous. Inside these traditional
tearooms, with their thick oak beams and
original sandstone walls, all three floors are
elegantly decorated, the ambience is warm
and friendly and the staff are eager to
please. After your delicious traditional tea,
why not take a gentle stroll around the
city walls?

CORNWALL
ROSKILLY'S
The Croust House
Tregellast Barton, St Keverne, Helston
TR12 6NX
Tel 01326 280479
Fax 01326 280320
e-mail admin@roskillys.co.uk
www.roskillys.co.uk

Opening hours 10.00am–5.30pm April–
October; 11.30am–5.00pm, weekends
only, November–March
**Cornish Cream Tea and extensive à la
carte menu**
Smoking permitted with discretion

Location From Helston, take Lizard Road; turn left towards St Keverne at roundabout at end of Culdrose airstation; after 14 kilometres (9 miles) take right-hand fork to Coverack; follow brown signs

Parking Own car park

Places of interest nearby Working family farm, craft shop; surrounding countryside is designated area of outstanding natural beauty

Two generations of the Roskilly family run this working farm, where every single aspect of the enterprise has been undertaken by them. The Croust House, as the delightful tearooms are known, was created out of the old milking parlour and calf pens. The organic Jersey herd has a new parlour, converted from a redundant Dutch barn and you can watch the cows being milked at 4.30pm one afternoon and over-indulge on the golden home-made clotted cream, ice cream, truffles and fudge the next! Rachel Roskilly's kitchen turns

out wonderful home-made food all day – the quiches are especially good, but tea is a must, even at 10.00am if that's what you fancy! Apart from the wonderful scones and cream, which are served with home-made preserves, there are three-layer cakes like coffee, cherry and brandy and crunchy caramel, cookies and tray bakes. Bagged teas include Earl and Lady Grey, Indian and Lapsang Souchong. A little off the beaten track, but well worth the detour.

TRENANCE COTTAGE TEA ROOM & GARDENS

Trenance Lane, Newquay TR7 2HX
Tel/Fax 01637 872034
e-mail robert@trenance-cottage.co.uk
www.trenance-cottage.co.uk

Opening hours 10.30am–5.00pm March–October; limited winter opening, please check (accommodation open all year round)

Set cream tea, extensive tea à la carte
Smoking permitted in garden only
Location From the town centre, follow Edgcumbe Avenue past the zoo and Waterworld, under viaduct, past Trenance Gardens into Trevemper Road; look out for boating lakes on the right; Trenance Cottage is opposite the lakes

Parking On-street parking nearby

Places of interest nearby Trenance Gardens, Heritage Cottages, Eden Project, Lost Gardens of Heligan, Tate Gallery, Hepworth Museum

What better place to enjoy a most exquisite tea than the idyllic surroundings of Trenance Cottage. Lovingly restored, the 200-year-old Georgian villa has been a tearoom since the 1920s. The tearooms and garden recapture the charm of a lost age, combined with excellent food, friendliness and professionalism. Local Cornish produce is used in abundance in the creation of the highest quality home-made fare – the delectable fruit or plain scones, hot saffron or yeast buns and cakes.

The tea gardens are a joy to behold, abounding with colourful flowers in summer and are the perfect place to linger over a cup of Assam or Earl Grey, Lapsang Souchong or Darjeeling.

CUMBRIA
KIRKSTONE GALLERIES
Chesters Café
Skelwith Bridge, nr Ambleside LA22 9NN
Tel/Fax 01539 432553
www.kirkstone-galleries.com

Opening hours 10.00am–5.00pm April–October; 10.00am–4.45pm November–March
Extensive tea à la carte menu
No smoking
Location By road, on the A593 between Ambleside and Coniston
Parking Gallery car park
Places of interest nearby Slate Quarry, Blackwell Arts and Crafts House, exploring the surrounding area of the Lake District

You'll find Chesters Café tucked inside the Kirkstone Galleries, which houses an exciting home furnishings emporium. The building was originally a bobbin mill, but this is where the past ends, for inside the emphasis is on contemporary living. The café itself is self-service which means you may have to queue at busy times but be patient, the wait is worthwhile. Daily specials are chalked up on huge blackboards and items get rubbed out as they run out; let this be a warning. If you see something that you really crave, take it then and there, for supplies may run out before you go back for your next course. There are no apologies for this from the management since everything is home-made using the freshest and purest ingredients and baking goes on all day long to keep up with demand; you can see the activity for yourself.

Tiers of tantalizing home-baked cakes – no secret recipes as such, simply old-fashioned family favourites – are displayed next to platters of scones and tea-breads, pavlovas and roulades. You might be tempted by the iced lemon sponge, layered with home-made lemon curd and topped with passion-fruit icing or the chocolate cake layered and topped with a glossy rich chocolate ganache. Alternatively you could settle for a sumptuous slice of pineapple, cherry and sultana cake. The atmosphere is bustly, the seating comfortable and the outside terraces, within earshot of Skelwith Force, positively delightful, especially if the sun shines. Whether you have made a diversion from Ambleside or are stopping whilst on a hike in the stunning Lakes, Chesters will not disappoint you. Nor will the gallery shop, which is bursting with all sorts of beautiful designer items, as well as tea from Farrer's of Harrogate.

SHARROW BAY COUNTRY HOUSE HOTEL

Lake Restaurant
Lake Ullswater, Penrith CA10 2LZ
Tel 01768 486301 (booking essential for non-residents)
Fax 01768 486349
e-mail enquiries@sharrow-bay.com
www.sharrow-bay.com

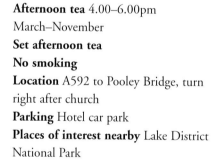

Afternoon tea 4.00–6.00pm
March–November
Set afternoon tea
No smoking
Location A592 to Pooley Bridge, turn right after church
Parking Hotel car park
Places of interest nearby Lake District National Park

The Sharrow Bay Hotel is a luxurious small hotel created over 50 years ago by an enterprising young man who was determined, against the odds, to make a personal dream come true. He fell in love with the stunning views of Lake Ullswater and the surrounding fells and the innumerable awards bestowed upon the hotel are a testimony to the great success of the venture.

Nothing about Sharrow Bay is understated: the décor is theatrical and sumptuous, there are wonderful fresh flowers everywhere and antiques and bric-a–brac are to be found in every corner. The ambience here is warm and welcoming, the service impeccable. Note that children under 13 years of age are not admitted at Sharrow Bay.

Don't have lunch beforehand, nor arrange to have another meal that day, for the assortment and quantity of delicacies served at tea are beyond your wildest imagination. Non-residents are served tea in the Lake Restaurant, seated at a table by the window. From this vantage point you can bask in the wonderful views whilst savouring delectable finger sandwiches, scones, teacakes and home-made cakes and pastries ranging from fruit cake, fruit tartlets, chocolate éclairs and iced lemon cake. The selection changes daily and what you don't manage to eat will be packed up in a box for you to take away and enjoy later. Your teapot, filled with Darjeeling, Lapsang Souchong, Keemun or other leaf tea will be kept warm under a delightful chintz tea cosy

---

DERBYSHIRE
THE OLD ORIGINAL BAKEWELL PUDDING SHOP

The Square, Bakewell DE45 1BT
Tel 01629 812193
Fax 01629 812260
www.bakewellpuddingshop.co.uk

Opening hours 9.00am–9.00pm
May–October; 9.00am–5.00pm
November–April
Two set teas Bakewell Cream Tea, Full
Afternoon Tea; tea à la carte also served
No smoking
No disabled access
Location Just off A6, in the Market Square
Parking Public car parks in local area
Places of interest nearby Evening tours of
the Pudding Shop; exploring the beautiful
Peak District, 5 kilometres (3 miles) from
Chatsworth and Haddon Hall

One thing you won't get at the Old
Original Bakewell Pudding Shop is the
secret recipe for the all-time favourite
Bakewell pudding. It has been hand-made
in the kitchens of this charming
seventeenth-century building for over 100
years and came about by accident, when, in
the 1860s, a local cook spread strawberry
jam over some pastry and then poured egg
mixture over the top before cooking it. The
result was an instant success and a Mrs
Wilson managed to obtain the recipe and
went into business making puddings. The
rest is history.

Feast your eyes on the wonderful
window display of larder goods as you
enter the shop and have a look at the huge
selection of cakes and breads before you
climb the stairs to the bustly first-floor
restaurant. Oak beams and antique copper
kitchen paraphernalia add to the feeling of
times past. Whether you have a traditional
set tea or order à la carte, make sure you
have a slice of Bakewell pudding, served as

it should be – hot with custard or cream.
Bagged teas on offer include Darjeeling and
Ceylon. Before you leave, why not buy a
pudding to take home?

DEVON
ROGER'S TEAROOM
49 Waterside Haven Road, Exeter
EX2 8GX
Tel 01392 433313
Opening hours 10.30am–5.30pm
Wednesday–Sunday during summer;
10.30am–5.00pm during winter; closed
Monday and Tuesday and all of January

Two set afternoon teas served all day
Roger's Traditional Full Tea, Cream Tea
No smoking
Location Follow signs for Exeter Quay
Parking No parking in immediate area
Places of interest nearby Within the
Exeter Quay and Canal Trust; tearooms are
overlooking historic canal basin

There is a lovely homely feeling about Roger's Tearoom, which occupies an enviable position on the historic Exeter Quay. It's light and airy but warm and cosy with its terracotta and mustard walls and eclectic mix of old oak and new furniture. Fresh flowers abound both inside and out, where on a good day you can sit in comfort under a glazed canopy, shielded from the sun by a huge umbrella. The Olvers, who are renowned for producing the most excellent home-made cakes, scones and savouries, serve tea beautifully using lovely china, some of which is decorated very appropriately with teacups and saucers and tiered cake stands. There are five varieties of scone to choose from – white, brown, sultana, date or apple – and Miranda's apple and ginger jam is the perfect accompaniment. As for the cakes and pastries, you'll go wild about the strawberry and raspberry gateau. For something more tame try the carrot and almond tart or a home-baked chocolate bourbon biscuit. The selection of leaf teas is good and includes Assam, Lady Grey and Darjeeling. This really is afternoon tea as it used to be.

DORSET
THE OLD TEA HOUSE
44 High West Street, Dorchester DT1 1UT
Tel 01305 263719

Opening hours 10.00am–5.00pm, Tuesday–Sunday May–September;

10.00am–4.00pm Wednesday–Sunday October–April; closed during January
Set Dorset Cream Tea or tea à la carte menu
No smoking
Location In the centre of town, on the main street, near Top-o-Town roundabout
Parking Public car park 50 metres (55 yards) away
Places of interest nearby Devon and Dorset Military Museum, Roman Town House, Thomas Hardy memorabilia in Dorset County Museum

There has been a tearoom here since 1902, but the picturesque, white-washed building, with its bay windows and striped

awnings, dates back to 1635. Inside is just what you would hope to find in a quintessentially English tearoom – inglenook fireplace, original beams, working gas lights and a warm, welcoming atmosphere. The walled garden is a tranquil haven for summer tea.

The Dorset Cream Tea is a favourite, choose one of four types of scones – plain, fruit, wholemeal and cheese. Don't miss the "naughty but nice" speciality Dorset Apple Cake – sponge, a layer of apple topped with crumble and served warm with clotted cream or ice cream to go with your beverage – the standard range is on offer here. The Old Tea House is unable to cater for special dietary requirements.

GLOUCESTERSHIRE
LORDS OF THE MANOR
Upper Slaughter, near Bourton-on-the Water, GL54 2JD
Tel 01451 820243
Fax 01451 820696
e-mail lordsofthemanor@btinternet.com
www.lordsofthemanor.com

Afternoon tea 3.30–5.30pm Monday– Saturday; 4.00–5.30pm Sunday
Two set teas Cream Tea, Full Afternoon Tea; also tea and biscuits
No smoking
Location Take A429 towards Stow-on-the Wold then turn towards The Slaughters and Lower Slaughter
Parking Hotel has own car park

Places of interest nearby Bourton-on-the Water, the Cotswolds, Kiftsgate and Hidcote Gardens, Sudeley Castle, Warwick Castle, Blenheim Palace

The poet Milton is reputed to have written his famous trilogy *Paradise Lost* at Eyford, just 1 kilometre (½ mile) upstream of Slaughter Brook, which meanders through the delightful grounds of the Lords of the Manor. The honey-coloured Cotswold stone house was once a rectory and parts of it date back to 1650. Inside, comfortable sofas, real fires, handsome antiques and family portraits add to the warm convivial atmosphere of a fine country house and it is a most agreeable place to enjoy a traditional afternoon tea.

There's a lovely terrace where you can take tea, weather permitting, or try one of the lounges, the drawing-room or bar. Whichever place you choose you'll be served graciously. It's all linen cloths and napkins, silver tea-ware and tiered cake-stands and you will drool over the very

fresh fruit scones, baked by the chef after lunch. Then you can indulge in the Sachertorte, carrot, rich Dundee or banana cake. If you are feeling really restrained you could settle for home-made biscuits and tea – the usual as well as the unusual, like Blue Flower Earl Grey perhaps.

KENT
COUNTY HOTEL
The Tea Room
High Street, Canterbury CT1 2RX
Tel 01227 766266
Fax 01227 451512
e-mail info@county.macdonald-hotels.co.uk
www.macdonaldhotels.co.uk

Opening hours 9.00am–8.00pm; tea served all day
Two set teas Traditional Afternoon Tea, Cream Tea; tea à la carte also available
Smoking permitted
Location Halfway down the pedestrianized High Street in city centre
Parking Hotel has own car park
Places of interest nearby Canterbury Cathedral, Canterbury Heritage Centre, Canterbury Tales, St Augustine's Abbey

The tearooms at The County are well known for serving a traditional old-style English cream tea and are the perfect place to recharge your batteries after a day's sightseeing in Chaucer's Canterbury. Rest in a comfortable armchair or squashy sofa, warm yourself by the open fire in winter

and soak up the atmosphere of the fifteenth-century room with its oak beams, evocative of a bygone age. Then you can tuck into the delicious afternoon tea, beautifully presented on a gilt three-tier stand and choose your cake or pastry from the mouth-watering selection of home-made goodies. For the hungry traveller, try the delicious traditional Welsh rarebit – very much a favourite with the locals.

NOTTINGHAMSHIRE
OLLERTON WATERMILL TEASHOP
Market Place, Ollerton, Newark
NG22 9AA
Tel 01623 824094/822469

Opening hours Tuesday–Sunday 10.30am–5.00pm March–October; 11.00am–4.00pm November; closed December–February
Tea à la carte or Ollerton Mill Cream Tea
No smoking
Disabled access Limited as the teashop is situated upstairs, but there is a small foyer table for two to three people on the ground floor
Location Ollerton lies at the junction of the A614 and B616, between Worksop and Nottingham; the Watermill is almost opposite the church
Parking In public village car park
Places of interest nearby Nottingham, Sherwood Forest, Ollerton Mill exhibition

Situated on the edge of Sherwood Forest is a tiny corner of rural England where you'll find the unspoilt village of Ollerton and where not much has changed for three centuries. There has been a mill on the spot since 1713 and its fascinating history gives visitors a peek at what life was like for a working miller in the eighteenth century. The ground floor of the red brick building boasts a 5-metre (16-foot) diameter waterwheel, dating from 1862 and Kate and Ellen Mettam's award-winning teashop is housed upstairs in the old millwright's workshop.

You get a splendid view of the waterwheel and mill race from the entrance and of the River Maun from the teashop. Simple furnishings – white-topped pine tables, pine chairs and whitewashed walls – complete the tranquil setting for a tea which is a truly old-fashioned event and a real treat. Delectable home-made food is the order of the day and as you might expect, the mill – restored and run by the Mettam husbands – produces all the finest milled flour used in the baking. Traditional scones – plain, cheese or wholemeal fruit – emerge from the ovens at regular intervals. Generous slices of wholesome cakes, like grandma used to make, include coffee and walnut, lemon and the very popular carrot cake are served. There's Bakewell tart or, for the totally indulgent, pavlova filled with fresh cream and fruit. Regular visitors are used to having their tea-tasting buds challenged by the "guest teas" which appear on the menu from time to time, but there is always a wide variety of bagged teas available, including Lapsang Souchong, Lady Grey and Assam available.

No visit for tea would be complete without a look at the exhibition which tells the story of Ollerton Mill from Doomsday England to the present day – truly living history. And if you are a home baker, then why not buy some Ollerton Mill flour on your way out?

OXFORDSHIRE
OLD PARSONAGE HOTEL
Parsonage Bar
1 Banbury Road, Oxford OX2 6NN
Tel 01865 310210 (bookings taken and preferred)
Fax 01865 311262
e-mail info@oldparsonage-hotel.co.uk
www.oxford-hotels-restaurants.co.uk

Afternoon tea 3.00–6.00pm
Set teas Traditional Afternoon Tea, Parson's Light Tea; tea à la carte also served
Smoking permitted

No disabled access

Location On Banbury Road, at north end of St Giles, next to St Giles Church; between Somerville and Keble Colleges

Parking Hotel has private car park

Places of interest nearby Colleges of Oxford University, punting on River Cherwell, Ashmolean Museum

A favourite with parents reviving the flagging spirits of their student offspring or hungry school children, the Old Parsonage has a well-deserved reputation for serving a very good, old-fashioned afternoon tea. The creeper-clad, honey-stoned seventeenth-century building has a remarkably colourful history. It has served as a safe haven for persecuted clergy, been a stronghold for Royalists and was even home to Oscar Wilde, the famed wit and member of the literati. The sense of the past is still evident inside, even though the hotel has been modernized. Old features have been retained and the ambience is that of a smart townhouse with panelling, comfortable leather chairs and walls covered in old prints. There is a delightful front terrace where you can enjoy tea, weather permitting.

Everything from the sandwiches to the scones – plain or cheese – to the cakes is home-baked and delicious. Quality leaf teas served in china pots include Lapsang Souchong, Darjeeling and the house Old Parsonage Blend. Owner Jeremy Mogford's philosophy is to give you the best and his staff ensure you have a wonderful time and enjoy a real treat.

STAFFORDSHIRE
GREYSTONES
23 Stockwell Street, Leek ST13 6DH
Tel/Fax 01538 398522

Opening hours 10.00am–5.00pm Wednesday, Friday and Saturday

Tea à la carte

No smoking

Disabled access Very limited

Location On the A523 from Macclesfield to Ashbourne, teashop is next to the library

Parking Public parking locally

Places of interest nearby Leek is a fine market town, famous for its antique shops and School of Embroidery; wonderfully scenic Peak District close at hand, as is Alton Towers

Taking tea at Greystones is like entering the home of very good friends who want to make your visit as relaxed and enjoyable as possible. The front parlour of Janet and

Roger Warrillow's elegant seventeenth-century house, with its mullioned windows, flagstone floors, wood panelling and walls adorned with old prints and paintings, is the setting for a most wonderful tea or lunchtime treat. But ponder a while on some local history before you order, for Leek, with its cobbled streets and restored water-powered corn mill, was once the centre of a flourishing silk industry. It was here that William Morris, the founder of the Arts and Crafts Movement, learned the art of dyeing and it was also home to the renowned Leek School of Embroidery.

The gentle chiming of the clock, evocative of a slower pace of life, adds to the tranquil atmosphere. Note that this is probably not the place to bring young children as there are no particular facilities for them or space inside for pushchairs. Eating is an absolute pleasure here. There are cheese, fruit or plain scones that positively melt in the mouth and cakes and sweets which people travel miles to enjoy. Particular teatime favourites from the kitchen at Greystones are Queen Mother's date and walnut sponge with toffee topping, carrot cake and apricot frangipane tart. Or try a slice of Grandma Birch's excellent gingerbread, which is made to a 100-year-old recipe. The range of bagged teas on offer is extensive and includes China Yunnan, Lapsang Souchong, Lady Grey and Earl Grey. Everything about Greystones is truly delightful and it's no wonder that its dedicated owners have won so many awards.

EAST SUSSEX
MOCK TURTLE TEA-SHOP
4 Pool Valley, Brighton BN1 1NJ
Tel 01273 327380

Opening hours 10.00am–6.00pm Tuesday–Saturday; check for Christmas and late spring closures
Set cream tea and huge à la carte menu
No smoking
Disabled access Two steps into shop, limited space inside
Location Close by The Lanes and The Royal Pavilion
Parking Voucher, meter and public car parks in town centre
Places of interest nearby The Lanes, Royal Pavilion, sea front

The Mock Turtle is really a country teashop in town and it has a very traditional feel about it. Whether you have just marvelled at the splendour of the Royal Pavilion, browsed through the antique shops in the nearby Lanes or had a bracing walk along the promenade and pier, the irresistible food will revive and restore you. Owners Gordon and Birthe Chater pride themselves on using only the freshest, highest quality ingredients, including locally-produced honey and cream. Everything, from the bread to the florentines and flapjacks, is prepared on the premises, often to their own recipes. Choose fluffy white or wholemeal scones, topped with butter, whipped cream and jam followed by one of the Mock Turtle's famous melt-in-the-mouth meringues filled with (more) cream and fresh seasonal fruit. There is a wide range of the finest loose leaf teas. Wholesome, homely and heavenly.

WEST SUSSEX
SHEPHERDS TEA ROOMS
35 Little London, Chichester PO19 2PL
Tel/Fax 01243 774761
www.teagifts.co.uk

Opening hours 9.15am–5.00pm Monday–Friday; 9.00am–5.00pm Saturday; closed all Bank holidays
Two set afternoon teas Shepherds Cream Tea, Traditional Cream Tea; extensive tea à la carte
No smoking
No disabled access
Location In city centre; Little London just off East Street
Parking Public car parks nearby
Places of interest nearby Goodwood House and Racecourse, South Downs, Chichester and harbour, Chichester Festival Theatre

Inside the lovely listed Georgian building off Chichester's busy high street is Shepherds. Oak floors, airy lemon and pale lime décor and personal service add to the calm atmosphere in which you can feast on an award-winning traditional tea and drink a very invigorating beverage.

You won't be able to resist the mouth-watering home-made scones – either fruit,

cheese or wholemeal – and be prepared to choose between five different preserves. Both strawberry and rhubarb or raspberry and redcurrant make a very refreshing change and are excellent topped with rich clotted cream. Then there are the hearty, wholesome cakes like the very popular Earl Grey tea-bread, orange and sultana slices or coffee and walnut cake. Frankly, you'll be spoilt for choice by the tempting display in the teashop. And if you are feeling quite hungry, then a savoury option of rarebit, the speciality of the house, is an absolute must. The biggest problem is deciding

which of the six unusual variations – maybe Stilton and Tomato or Hawaiian – to order. There's the usual range of leaf teas, as well as Pure Assam and some green teas. Their teas can be ordered in the tearooms or via the internet and be sent throughout the world. A very "English" tea indeed, in a quintessentially English teashop.

WARWICKSHIRE

BENSONS

4 Bards Walk, Stratford-upon-Avon
CV37 6EY
Tel 01789 261116
Fax 01789 294378
e-mail bensons-byre@compuserve.com
www.bensonsofstratford.co.uk

Opening hours 8.00am–5.30pm
Monday–Saturday; during summer open
11.00am–4.30pm Sunday
Two set afternoon teas Full Traditional,
Champagne Tea; extensive tea à la carte
No smoking
Location Two minutes walk from
Shakespeare's Birthplace on Henley Street,
opposite main post office
Parking Public car parks in town centre
Places of interest nearby Shakespeare's
birthplace, Anne Hathaway's Cottage,
Swan Theatre

From the outside of Bensons, with its
restored nineteenth-century façade, you
might expect to find a quaint, old-
fashioned tearoom. Instead, you are treated
to a light and airy contemporary
conservatory-style interior, abundant with
flowers, foliage and original watercolours.
The calm and relaxing ambience is
wonderful and a complete contrast to the
busy world outside. And all this before you
have sampled the gourmet tea!

Bensons works closely with the
internationally renowned Maison Blanc,
originally established by leading chef,

Raymond Blanc and the daily changing
selection of hand-made patisserie on offer
is simply divine. Just imagine *Millefeuille
Framboise* – layers of caramelized *pâte
feuilletée* with *crème mousseline* and fresh
raspberries – and you'll know what I mean!
For the less adventurous, the traditional
afternoon tea of freshly prepared
sandwiches, warm scone with clotted cream
and conserve will not fail to please. Extra
special is the Champagne Tea, for you are
served a half-bottle of fine, chilled house
bubbly alongside the tea sandwiches,
scones, afternoon pastries and traditional
fruit cake. The quality and presentation of
food at Bensons is exemplary and it has to
be one of Stratford-upon-Avon's best kept
secrets. It comes as no surprise that it is a
multi award-winner.

WILTSHIRE

THE BRIDGE TEA ROOMS

24A Bridge Street, Bradford-on-Avon
BA15 1BY
Tel 01225 865537

Opening hours 9.30am–5.00pm,
Monday–Friday; 9.30am–5.30pm
Saturday; 10.30am–5.30pm, Sunday;
closed Xmas Day and Boxing Day
Three set teas Queen Victoria's Glorious
Champagne Tea, The Famous Bridge
Cream Tea, The Bridge Full Afternoon Tea;
extensive à la carte menu
No smoking
No disabled access

Location Near public library on
St Margaret's Street side of bridge
Parking Public car park by tearooms
Places of interest nearby Saxon church,
fourteenth-century tithe barn, Wiltshire
countryside

This award-winning tearoom, originally
built in 1675 as a blacksmith's cottage,
oozes character with its tiny windows and
low entrance. Hanging baskets and window
boxes are a blaze of colour in the summer.
The interior is a bit of a surprise, for it is
reminiscent of the Victorian age, complete
with the aspidistra plant, commemorative
china and a picture of the great Queen
herself gazing down on you from the wall.
The friendly waitresses, in their long black
dresses, frilly white aprons and starched
mop caps, could easily have walked out of
the original ABC teashop on London
Bridge. Add to this the delightful views of
the thirteenth-century town bridge and you
know that you are in for a treat.

Francine Whale, the inspired creator of
this truly nostalgic tearoom, is an absolute
star of the culinary arts. The cakes and

bakes which she creates on a daily basis are
luscious – try chocolate cheesecake, a
creamy roulade, banana gateau or rich fruit
cake and, of course, the scones for which
Mrs Whale is famous. The royal influence
is evident in Queen Victoria's Glorious
Champagne Tea – feast on smoked salmon
sandwiches, strawberries and cream, fat
scones with cream and strawberry preserve
and half a bottle of bubbly. But you could
make do with the Famous Bridge Cream
Tea or, if you dare, the Bridge Full
Afternoon Tea – sandwiches, a crumpet, a
huge scone with cream and preserve and
cake. To quench your thirst there are some
very special leaf teas. Darjeeling FOP,
Ceylon Superior BOP, First Flush
Darjeeling, Pelham and more are sure to
please the most discerning tea-drinker.

WORCESTERSHIRE
TISANES
Cotswold House, 21 The Green, Broadway
WR12 7AA
Tel/Fax 01386 852112
e-mail tisanes@clara.co.uk
www.tisanes.co.uk

Opening hours 10.00am–5.00pm
Monday–Saturday, 10.30am–5.00pm
Sunday, July–end October and every school
holiday; other times tearoom closed
Thursdays; shop 10.00am–5.30pm
Tea à la carte
No smoking except in garden
No disabled access

Location In Broadway High Street, overlooking The Green and the War Memorial
Parking Public car park 180 metres (200 yards) through arcade at rear of shop
Places of interest nearby Broadway, Snowshill Manor, Hidcote Manor, Sudeley Castle, Cotswolds

Now here is a traditional teashop with a very continental touch, right in the heart of one of the Cotswolds' most popular villages. The warm sandstone, bow-windowed, building dates back to the fifteenth century and the old-fashioned feeling is evident in the shop and the tearoom. You have to pass through the shop, which positively bulges with the hundreds of different novelty teapots which Tisanes is famous for – all for sale – as well as a large range of tea-related gifts.

Taking tea is a serious business here, for besides the glorious home-baked scones, teacakes, cakes, gateaux and desserts on display – try Apple Janette (a confection of apples, fruit and almonds in a sponge base

on top of pastry), or coffee and chocolate pyramid – there are 26 varieties of leaf tea on offer. Darjeeling Vintage is undoubtedly the most prized and expensive, but it's a small price to pay for such an exquisite beverage. All the teas can be purchased in the shop or ordered by post. Note that children are welcome and can be accommodated, but there is no room inside for pushchairs, prams or high chairs due to the nature of the building.

YORKSHIRE
BETTYS CAFÉ TEAROOMS
1 Parliament Street, Harrogate HG1 2QU
Tel 01423 877300
Fax 01423 877307
www.bettysandtaylors.com
www.bettysbypost.com

Opening hours 9.00am–9.00pm
Two set afternoon teas Bettys Traditional, Cream Tea; extensive tea à la carte menu
Smoking permitted in designated areas
Location Bettys is situated in the town centre on the main Leeds to Ripon route; the tearooms stand at the top of Montpelier Hill
Parking Metered parking readily-available locally
Places of interest nearby Old Pump Rooms, Turkish Baths, Harlow Carr Botanical Gardens, gateway to the Dales

Lady Raine Spencer once drooled over Bettys, praising it for being better than any of the hundreds of teashops she and her

range of products, including pottery mugs and teapots. Just thinking about this rich fruity scone, made with citrus peel, almonds and cherries, makes my taste buds tingle. Bettys Craft Bakery is the creative heart of the business and everything, from the pikelets (a Yorkshire crumpet) and tea-loaves to the amazing array of cakes and patisserie is hand-baked there. You get a good idea of how the Swiss Alps meets the Yorkshire Dales with the choice between a super rich Swiss Chocolate Torte and a traditional Yorkshire Curd Tart. You are truly spoilt for choice.

The tea served at Bettys comes from their sister company, the renowned tea merchants, Taylors of Harrogate. Order either of the two set teas and you'll be served the excellent Tea Room Blend Tea, but for the aficionado there are speciality teas to dream about. Ceylon Blue Sapphire, Special Estate Darjeeling or Tippy Assam as well as China Rose Petal and "Good Luck" Green Tea are on the list and these and many more are on sale in the shop – along with the Fat Rascal pottery mugs! There are also branches of Bettys in Ilkley, Northallerton and York.

husband had visited in cities all over the world. Few people could disagree with this sentiment for Bettys has earned a worldwide reputation for excellence since it was founded, in Harrogate, in 1919, by an adventurous and talented Swiss ancestor of the present owners. The Harrogate teashop, with its art deco mirrors, panelling, oak staircase and picture windows overlooking Montpelier Gardens and The Stray, is an oasis of calm and elegance and is on any tourist's list of places to visit. Like all the branches, it is the very epitome of Yorkshire warmth and hospitality.

Of all the delicious food served at Bettys it's the Yorkshire Fat Rascal that is the most famous – so much so that it has its own

LITTLE BETTYS
46 Stonegate, York YO1 2AS
Tel 01904 622865
Fax 01904 640348
www.bettysandtaylors.com
www.bettysbypost.com
byp@bettysandtaylors.co.uk

Afternoon tea 3.00–5.30pm
Two set teas Bettys Traditional, Cream
Tea; extensive tea à la carte menu
Smoking permitted in designated areas
Disabled access To downstairs shop only
Location In central pedestrian area, two
minutes walk from York Minster
Parking Public car park in Bootham Row
Places of interest nearby York City Art
Gallery, York Minster, Jorvik Viking
Centre, National Railway Museum,
Museum Gardens, Barly Hall

Warm and comforting, Little Bettys is
tucked away in medieval Stonegate, one of
York's most famous streets, a step away
from the Minster. This charming tea place
was one of the original "kiosks" opened by
Taylors of Harrogate, now Bettys sister
company, at the turn of the century, and
continues to serve a refreshing cup of tea.

The small, well-stocked, ground floor
shop is a gem, furnished using traditional
materials including oak and marble. Loose
tea is sold out of large urns, so there is no
need to go home without a "souvenir". The
upstairs tearoom, with its beams and
fireplaces, lends a sense of timelessness to
the surroundings.

The food served at Bettys is wholesome
and homely and has a worldwide
reputation for excellence. Southerners often
bemoan the lack of a Bettys nearer home,
but I doubt it would be the same. The
famous Fat Rascal somehow belongs in
Yorkshire, as does their scrumptious curd
tart and vanilla slice. Long live Bettys.

TREASURER'S HOUSE TEA ROOMS
Minster Yard, York YO1 7JL
Tel 01904 646757
Fax 01904 647372
e-mail yorkth@smtp-ntrust.org.uk

Opening hours 11.00am–4.30pm (last
orders), closed Friday late March–end
October
Three set teas House Party Tea, Butler's
Tea, Yorkshire High Tea; tea à la carte menu
No smoking
Disabled access Limited, but refreshments
can be served on the ground floor by
request
Location Signposted around York Minster
Parking City centre car parks
Places of interest nearby York City Art
Gallery, York Minster, Jorvik Viking

Centre, National Railway Museum, Museum Gardens, Barley Hall

You may be "below stairs" here, ensconced in that intriguing part of every grand house which was inhabited by an army of servants, but you certainly get a true sense of the history of the splendid Treasurers House by being here. Set in the shadow of York Minster, the last owner of the house was an Edwardian gentleman by the name of Frank Green, who was passionate about good food. He would undoubtedly have approved of the cosy and welcoming atmosphere of the National Trust tearooms which visitors flock to for its home-baking. The Yorkshire lemon tart and lemon curd tart make your tongue tingle and the toasted crumpets drip with melting butter. Have a set tea, all served with a strong cup of Yorkshire brew or, for a more filling feast, have the Yorkshire High Tea. The shop also sells tea for you to take home.

SCOTLAND

FIFE

KIND KYTTOCK'S KITCHEN
Cross Wynd, Falkland KY15 7BE
Tel 01337 857477
Fax 01337 857379

Afternoon tea 2.00–5.30pm, closed Mondays and for two weeks from Christmas Day
Two set teas Cream Tea, Afternoon Tea; large à la carte menu

No smoking
Location At the centre of Falkland near the palace, turn up at the square into Cross Wynd
Parking On-street parking opposite

Places of interest nearby Falkland Palace, Garden and Old Burgh

Kind Kyttock was a woman who, legend has it, served food to weary travellers passing through the area. The establishment named after her is so popular with locals and visitors that if you arrive later than 10.45am on a Sunday morning, you'll be hard pushed to find a table. Sandwiched in the middle of an early eighteenth century terrace, the interior is cosy and comforting, especially when the open fire is roaring on a cold winter's day. Dark furniture and bright tablecloths add to the charming traditional feel. Whatever you choose from the menu, be it the scones or Scot's pancakes (drop scones), the deliciously sweet Campbell Fudge Cake, date shortbread or any of the other delectable items on offer, the homely food will leave a lingering impression. You'll be served an excellent brew of leaf tea from the range on offer which includes Golden Ceylon, Pure China and Russian. It's no wonder that this lovely teashop has won so many awards.

MIDLOTHIAN

CALEDONIAN HOTEL

The Lounge
Princes Street, Edinburgh EH1 2AB
Tel 0131 222 8888
Fax 0131 222 8889
www.hilton.com

Afternoon tea 3.00–5.30pm
Two set teas Traditional Afternoon Tea, Celebration Tea
Smoking permitted
Location On the west end of Princes Street, at the bottom of Lothian Road
Parking Private car park
Places of interest nearby Edinburgh Castle, Palace of Holyrood House, The Royal Mile, Edinburgh Zoo, Princes Street designer shopping, Royal Yacht Britannia, Royal Botanic Garden, Scotch Whisky Heritage Centre

The Caledonian has been a landmark on the Edinburgh skyline for over 100 years

and no other venue quite captures the breathtaking view of Edinburgh Castle as this grand Edwardian hotel does. Taking tea in the Lounge is relaxing and restorative and the atmosphere is one of refined and sumptuous elegance. Tradition here dictates that besides the familiar finger sandwiches, scones and tea pastries, all of which are quite delicious, you are treated to drop scones (warm pancakes), clotted cream and a selection of preserves. It's a good idea to ask the waitress to bring the scones and pancakes after you have finished your sandwiches, so they are served to you warm. At weekends, you have the added pleasure of the resident pianist playing light classical music.

CLARINDA'S TEAROOM

69 Canongate, Royal Mile, Edinburgh
EH8 8BT
Tel 0131 557 1888

Opening hours 9.00am–4.45pm Monday –Saturday; 10.00am–4.45pm Sunday
Tea à la carte
No smoking
No disabled access
Location On the Royal Mile
Places of interest nearby Palace of Holyrood House, Scottish Parliament Building, People's Museum, Edinburgh Museum

The story goes that Clarinda (Agnes Maclehose 1759–1841) was a friend and mentor to Robert Burns, Scotland's most famous poet and the inspiration for his popular love song *Ae Fond Kiss*. The teashop named after her is very traditional inside – all lace tablecloths and Victorian bric-a-brac, some of which is for sale. Note that there is limited space for pushchairs and no high chairs are available.

Excellent home-cooked food emerges from the kitchen here and you'll be served very traditional teatime treats including scones and cream, rock cakes, banana bread and other favourites. The day's selection is displayed on the wooden trolley for you to choose from. Leaf tea includes Scottish Breakfast and Japanese Green. Value for money, Clarinda's is hard to beat and is a very cosy place to take tea.

Situated right in the heart of Glencoe village, against the backdrop of the Scottish Highlands' most breathtaking scenery and beautiful landscapes is Mrs Matheson's tearooms. You only have to be told that the proprietor is known far and wide as the "cake lady" to realise that you are in for a special treat. Visitors and locals alike are tempted by the welcoming aromas of freshly-baked scones and other home-made delights which drift from Mrs Matheson's kitchen. From a store of secret recipes she bakes, using local produce, a honey and whisky cake "to die for", and a chocolate cake described as "*extraordinaire*"; the strawberry shortcake isn't bad either. Try any of these after a energetic hike in the Highlands and you'll truly be in culinary heaven.

STRATHCLYDE
MRS MATHESON'S
Glencoe Village, West Highlands, Argyll PA39 4HP
Tel 01855 811590
Fax 01855 821322
e-mail anne.matheson@btinternet.com
www.mrsmathesons-glencoe.com

Afternoon tea 2.00–5.00pm; High tea 5.00–6.30pm; April–October
A la carte menu
No smoking
Location On main street, centre of village
Parking Own car park
Places of interest nearby Exploring the beautiful West Highlands

---

THE WILLOW TEA ROOMS
217 Sauchiehall Street, Glasgow G2 3EX
Tel/Fax 0141 332 0521
e-mail anne@willowtearooms.co.uk
www.willowtearooms.co.uk

Also at: 97 Buchanan Street, Glasgow G1 3HF, telephone 0141 204 5242 for opening hours.

Opening hours 9.30am–5.00pm Monday–Saturday; 12.00 noon–4.00pm Sunday and Bank holidays
Two set teas Cream Tea, Afternoon Tea; huge tea à la carte menu
Smoking permitted
No disabled access (tearoom on first floor)

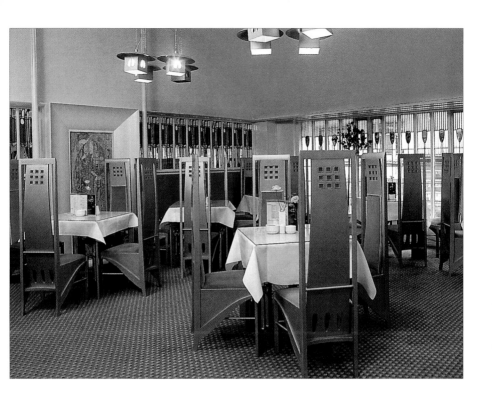

Location Centre of Glasgow
Parking Public car parks nearby
Places of interest nearby Burrell
Collection, Scotland Street School
Museum, Glasgow School of Art,
Hunterian Art Gallery

You really are stepping back in time to the
early 1900s when you take tea at the Willow
Tea Rooms, for this art nouveau treasure is a
wondrous recreation of the original which
Charles Rennie Mackintosh, the famed
architect and artist, designed and built for
his client, Kate Cranston, in 1903. Now, as
then, the main attraction, other than the
glorious food, is the Room de Luxe,
resplendent with silver furniture and leaded

mirror friezes, much of which was rescued
from the dismantled shop after it closed in
1928. The chairs, tables and lights have all
been recreated to the original designs. Anne
Mulhern, the proprietrix, has certainly
managed to capture the feeling of a bygone
age, for the pace here is unhurried and the
service superior.

There is such an extensive menu that you
can eat all day long if you want, with lots
of Scottish savoury dishes to choose from.
All the old favourite traditional tea food is
here, and, amongst the array of cakes and
pastries, are Sinful Chocolate Slice, which
rather speaks for itself, and Empire biscuit,
a double layer of shortbread sandwiched
with jam and dusted with icing sugar.

Anne's own massive chewy meringues are amazing and by far the most popular treat. When it comes to tea, the beverage list is extensive and includes Gunpowder Green and Russian Caravan, as well as a total of 13 herbal and fruit teas. Taking tea here is a unique experience and one not to be missed. A range of souvenirs are available to buy including prints of the exterior of the building, fine bone china mugs and bags or caddies of tea.

WALES
GLAMORGAN
THE MUSEUM OF WELSH LIFE
Gwalia Tea Rooms
St Fagans, Cardiff CF5 6XB
Tel/Fax 029 2056 6985

Opening hours 10.00am–5.00pm except Xmas day, Boxing Day and New Years Day
Set tea and extensive tea à la carte menu
No smoking
Location Exit 33 off M4, follow signs to the Museum of Welsh Life; tearooms are in grounds of museum (free admission to museum)
Parking Museum car park
Places of interest nearby Cardiff Castle, Cardiff Bay, Brecon Beacons

Traditional home-made Welsh teatime treats such as bara brith, teisen lap and Welsh cakes all appear on the menu of the glorious Gwalia Tea Rooms, set within the grounds of Cardiff's Museum of Welsh Life. Taking tea in this delightful establishment is to step back in time to the art deco period of the 1920s, for the tearoom is on the first floor of the Gwalia Stores, a local department store which has been reconstructed, stone by stone, within the museum. Traditional afternoon tea here includes dainty sandwiches, a Welsh cake and a warm scone, but you can always go à la carte and tuck into a slightly spiced and fruity Gwalia rock cake or a custard slice, another favourite on the menu. You've an extensive choice of some 40 leaf teas, including Oolong, Yunnan, Gunpowder and Rose Pouchong.

In case you are wondering, bara brith is a traditional Welsh fruit-bread, that has a heavy mixed fruit content and a fine blend of mixed spices. Welsh cakes are small and pastry-based, made to a traditional recipe of currants and mixed spices, lightly toasted on a griddle. Teisen lap means "cake plate" and is a slice of lightly fruited sponge cake which has been cooked on a plate rather than in a tin. Mike Morton can arrange to send you some Welsh cakes or bara brith if you find yourself suffering from withdrawal symptoms.

LLANDUDNO
ST TUDNO HOTEL
Promenade, Llandudno LL30 2LP
Tel 01492 874411
Fax 01492 860407
e-mail sttudnohotel@btinternet.co.uk
www.st-tudno.co.uk

Afternoon tea 2.30–5.30pm
Two set teas Welsh Afternoon Tea,
De Luxe Afternoon Tea
Smoking permitted in designated areas
Disabled access Limited
Location On the promenade, opposite the
pier entrance and gardens
Parking Hotel car park
Places of interest nearby Conwy and
Caernarfon Castle, Budnant Gardens,
Snowdonia National Park, Anglesey

There is something very special about
taking tea at St Tudno's. This seaside hotel
and its afternoon tea, have received heaps
of awards and once you have sampled the
warm hospitality, comfort and luxury you'll
understand why. It doesn't matter whether
you are cosily settled in the sitting room
with its delightful views of the seafront,
ensconced in one of the comfortable
lounges or watching the world go by from
the front terrace, your tea will be served in
style. Fine Wedgwood china, crisp linen
tablecloths and napkins add to the feeling
of quiet refinement.

The set teas combine tradition –
sandwiches, scones with cream and jam
and cake – with the local specialities of
bara brith and Welsh cakes. Generous slices
of coffee and walnut, Victoria sponge or
chocolate fudge are just some of the cakes
served with tea. The De Luxe tea includes
all of this plus smoked salmon, strawberries
and cream and a glass of champagne and it
is quite a struggle to get through all of the
delicious home-made food.

The quality and selection of teas is
equally impressive, with some 17 varieties
to choose from. The attention to detail
here is most impressive – from the silver,
tiered cake-stands to the choice of
skimmed, semi-skimmed or whole milk for
your tea.

Picture Credits

Index